Hector MacEacken
May '69.

PENGUIN PLAYS

PL55

CALIGULA and CROSS PURPOSE

ALBERT CAMUS

CALIGULA
and
CROSS PURPOSE

Translated by Stuart Gilbert

INTRODUCED BY

John Cruickshank

PENGUIN BOOKS

In association with Hamish Hamilton

Penguin Books Ltd, Harmondsworth, Middlesex, England
Penguin Books Pty Ltd, Ringwood, Victoria, Australia

—

Le Malentendu and *Caligula* first
published by Gallimard 1944
This translation first published by
Hamish Hamilton 1948
Published in Penguin Books 1965

—

—

Made and printed in Great Britain
by Western Printing Services Ltd, Bristol
Set in Monotype Baskerville

—

Contents

Introduction

Albert Camus was born at Mondovi, in the Constantine department of Algeria, on 7 November 1913. He was the second son of Lucien Camus, an impoverished agricultural worker of Alsatian origin, and Catherine Sintès, a woman of Spanish descent whose family settled in Algeria before 1870. Within a year of Camus's birth his father was killed in Europe during the first battle of the Marne and Madame Camus moved with her two small sons to the home of her own widowed mother in the Belcourt district of Algiers. She worked as a charwoman to help support her family, and during their early years Albert and his brother were looked after by their rather tyrannical grandmother. Camus's first published collection of essays, *L'Envers et l'endroit*, contains descriptions of the house and the district in which he grew up, together with portraits of his mother, his grandmother, and an uncle.

In 1918 Camus entered the *école communale* or primary school for the Belcourt district. Here he was fortunate in having a teacher, Louis Germain, who saw his intellectual promise and helped him to win a scholarship to the Lycée d'Alger in 1923 (thirty-five years later it was to Germain that Camus dedicated his speech accepting the Nobel Prize for Literature – his *Discours de Suède* published in 1958). Between 1923 and 1930, as a gifted young *lycéen*, he gradually developed those intellectual and sporting interests which he retained throughout his life. By the time he passed the *baccalauréat* in 1930 he was reading Gide, Montherlant, and Malraux. From 1928 to 1930 he kept goal for the football team, Racing Universitaire d'Alger. The year 1930 proved, in fact, to be a critical one in Camus's life. It was at this point that he experienced the first of several severe attacks of tuberculosis. As a result, his educational career was interrupted and his footballing activities had to stop; he found the latter consequence particularly hard to bear. Considerations of health also made it imperative that he should leave the small, dark, two-roomed apartment that had been his home for fifteen years. After a short period spent with an uncle who was a butcher by trade and a Voltairean republican by conviction, Camus decided to live on his own. He supported himself by a variety of jobs which included giving private lessons, selling spare parts for cars, working for the Meteorological Institute, and acting as a clerk both in the *préfecture* in Algiers and in an import–export business.

Camus was now registered as a philosophy student at the University of Algiers. At this time he came under another decisive influence – that of Jean Grenier, who encouraged, as a teacher, his interest in literature and philosophy, while sharing his enthusiasm for football. Later, in 1937, Camus was to dedicate *L'Envers et l'endroit* to Grenier. It was also during his student days that he experienced two very different and equally short love-affairs. The first was with Simone Hie, the daughter of an Algiers doctor, whom he married in 1933. This marriage was dissolved within a year. The second short love-affair was with the Algerian Communist Party, which he joined in 1934 and left for good in 1935 after doing propaganda work among the Moslem population. He resigned because, during Laval's visit to Moscow, Stalin was persuaded to order the French Communist Party to withdraw much of its support for the social and political demands of the Moslems. For Camus, this sudden change of policy meant a dramatic confrontation with the demands of a political expediency which he found contemptible. Several of his later writings, particularly *L'Homme révolté* (*The Rebel*), show how deeply he was affected by this experience.

During this time Camus managed to complete his *licence* at the University and he went on, in 1936, to obtain the *diplôme d'études supérieures* for a thesis on the relations between Hellenism and Christianity (and more particularly on the influence of Plotinus on St Augustine). A year later he had another attack of tuberculosis; he was prevented from taking the *agrégation* and his university career came to an end. He had to rest in the French Alps (his first visit to Europe) and returned to Algeria via Florence, Pisa, and Genoa.

It was two years earlier, in 1935, that Camus's deep love for the theatre found its first active expression. With a number of young left-wing intellectuals he played a prominent part in founding the so-called Théâtre du Travail in Algiers, whose aim, according to its manifesto, was to create a 'popular' theatre which would also be a 'school of values'. The intention was to bring good plays to the working population and to a small, progressive intellectual *élite*. Before long the Théâtre du Travail became the Théâtre de l'Équipe. It continued to proclaim its social mission, while adhering to the general conception of theatrical presentation insisted on by Copeau in Paris – that is, the emphasis was on the text and the acting, with relatively little attention paid to the décor. It was in these conditions that Camus, with the cooperation of his friends, wrote *Révolte dans les Asturies* with its subtitle: 'Essai de création collective, dédié aux victimes de répression.' The subject of this 'collective play' was the capture of Oviedo by the Asturian miners in 1934, their later defeat, and the executions which followed. It was published by Charlot in 1936 with financial help from the Amis du Théâtre du Travail.

Camus was soon deeply involved in the additional career of journalism. In 1938 he accepted Pascal Pia's offer of a post as *rédacteur-reporter* with the newly-founded left-wing newspaper *Alger-Républicain*. *Alger-Républicain* was anti-colonialist, supported the Popular Front, and campaigned vigorously for social justice in Algeria until it ceased publication in October 1939. For Camus this was a period of apprenticeship in journalism during which he acted variously as leader-writer, sub-editor, social and political reporter, and book-reviewer. The experience gained was immensely valuable when he undertook the editorship of the Parisian daily, *Combat*, which first appeared clandestinely in 1943. Among the books he reviewed for *Alger-Républicain* were Sartre's *La Nausée* and *Le Mur*. One of the most impressive of his social reports was a series of articles on the Moslems of the Kabylia region of Algeria. They were eventually republished, in abridged form, in *Actuelles III* (1958).

When the Second World War broke out in 1939 Camus had published two collections of essays (*L'Envers et l'endroit* and *Noces*) and a 'collective' play (*Révolte dans les Asturies*). He had completed another play, *Caligula*, but this was neither performed nor published at the time. He began writing *L'Étranger* (*The Outsider*) in 1939, and when he finished it in 1940 he went on to complete his first long essay on ideas, *Le Mythe de Sisyphe*, over a period of about six months. Both books were published by Gallimard in 1942 but were not widely noticed at the time. It was also in 1942, after periods spent alternately in Algeria and France, that Camus joined Pascal Pia, Claude Bourdet, and others in the 'Combat' resistance group and worked for the underground press.

After the Liberation, Camus immediately resumed his work in the theatre. In May 1944, before the actual liberation of Paris, the Théâtre des Mathurins had put on *Le Malentendu* (*Cross Purpose*) and it was published, along with *Caligula*, shortly afterwards. Maria Casarès and Marcel Herrand played Martha and Jan, but despite their talents

Le Malentendu did not have a good press. Among other things, it was too original and too disturbing to be quickly understood and accepted, though it had a more favourable reception when produced again in October of the same year. In the autumn of 1945 the Théâtre Hébertot put on *Caligula* (seven years after it was written) with Gérard Philipe in the title role. This time Camus scored a success: the play ran for over two hundred performances and has been successfully revived in France on a number of occasions since. Yet Camus's subsequent career as a dramatist was a chequered one. In 1948 he completed a play, *L'État de siège*, on the theme of a plague, symbolically interpreted. *L'État de siège* was a failure despite Barrault's resourceful production at the Marigny and a brilliant cast which included Barrault, Madeleine Renaud, Maria Casarès, and Brasseur. On the other hand, *Les Justes* was enthusiastically received when put on at the Hébertot in December 1949 with Serge Reggiani and Maria Casarès as Kaliaev and Dora. I think a quite strong case can be made for regarding *Les Justes* as Camus's finest dramatic achievement. In this country, however, it has generally been thought inferior to *Caligula*.

Camus wrote no other plays, but he had an increasingly successful career as a translator and adaptor for the stage. Nineteen fifty-nine saw what was probably his greatest achievement in this field – a brilliant stage version of Dostoyevsky's *The Possessed* at the Théâtre Antoine.

During these post-war years Camus also maintained a steady output of novels, essays, and political articles. In the sphere of fiction he followed *L'Étranger* with *La Peste* (*The Plague*) in 1947, *La Chute* (*The Fall*) in 1956, and a collection of short stories, *L'Exil et le royaume* (*Exile and the Kingdom*) in 1957. In 1945 his four *Lettres à un ami allemand* had been published in one small volume. They were followed by

L'Homme révolté in 1951, *L'Été* in 1954, *Réflexions sur la peine capitale* (his book against capital punishment written with Arthur Koestler) in 1957, and *Discours de Suède* (1958) containing both his speech accepting the Nobel Prize for Literature and a lecture on the writer and his time given four days later at the University of Uppsala. Much of his political journalism was reprinted in the three volumes of *Actuelles* which appeared in 1950, 1953, and 1958.

In 1957, at the early age of forty-four, Camus was awarded the Nobel Prize for Literature. He reacted to this distinction with characteristic modesty, saying that had he been a member of the committee he would have voted for Malraux. One can say that the award was widely welcomed, in France and overseas, yet it also provided an occasion for a number of Camus's French critics to attack his attitude to the burning question of Algeria. On the face of it, it seemed surprising that he should not have expressed himself clearly and publicly on such notorious matters as the torture of Djamila Boupacha, the murder of Maurice Audin, and indeed the whole conception and use of torture by many elements in the French army. On the other hand, facts which go some way towards explaining Camus's cautious and negative attitude should be borne in mind. For one thing, he himself belonged by birth and upbringing to the underprivileged 'European' population of Algeria – the most virulent source of anti-Moslem feeling. Again, his aged mother lived in Algiers and he made it clear that in any conflict between devotion to justice and devotion to his mother it would be his mother he would choose. In fact he faced and made this choice in so far as he feared for his mother's safety. It should also be said that Camus, unlike many of his critics, had drawn attention to the plight of the Moslem population as early as 1939, though he never saw the problems of his country in simple and straightforward 'colonialist' terms. He believed French technical and economic aid to be essential to its well-being and wanted what he called 'an Algerian Algeria . . . not an Egyptian Algeria'. Hence his visit to Algeria in 1956, his appeal for a truce, and his support of the ineffectual 'truce committees' formed in several parts of the country immediately afterwards. In his whole attitude to the Algerian war he remained on what for many of his admirers was the very unsatisfactory level of rather innocuous moral generalities. He appeared to be confirming those accusations of political otherworldliness which Sartre had made during their famous controversy and rupture of 1951.

Although he had expressed fears about an eventual 'Egyptian Algeria', Camus was not to witness the aftermath of Algerian independence in 1962. On Monday 4 January 1960, travelling at speed between Sens and Paris in a Facel-Véga driven by his friend and publisher Michel Gallimard, he met sudden death at the age of forty-six when the car skidded, hit two plane trees and was virtually cut in half. Part of the irony lies in the fact that Camus disliked cars and had intended to return to Paris by train until Gallimard persuaded him to change his mind (the return half of a rail ticket to Paris was found in his pocket). Part of the tragedy lies in the fact that he had written as recently as 1958, in the preface to a new edition of *L'Envers et l'endroit*: 'I continue to be convinced that my work hasn't even been begun.'

*

Much was written immediately after Camus's death about the appropriateness of its circumstances for a so-called 'prophet of the absurd'. To see Camus's work and ideas only in this light, however, is to see them very partially and to ignore much that is most moving and most noble in his achievement. It is true, of course, that at a certain period in his life (during which he wrote *Caligula* and *Le Malentendu*) he was very much preoccupied with what he called 'the absurd'. By this expression he meant what is inexplicable in terms of human reason: those experiences that defy rational explanation or seem to confound and controvert our sense of fair play, our desire for happiness, our need to find pattern and purpose in existence. He writes in *Le Mythe de Sisyphe* of such evidences of the absurd as the deadening routine of much modern industrial life; a sudden, unbidden questioning of the purpose of existence and the meaning of the lives we lead; the sense that time is rapidly and inexorably bearing us towards physical disintegration; the consciousness of our brief human lives in contrast to the endurance of inanimate nature; the 'otherness' of people and even of an element in ourselves; the waste of so much human potential in apparently arbitrary sudden death or protracted suffering.

To the extent to which he not only observed some such outlook among his contemporaries but shared it himself, Camus became for a time a symptom and a spokesman for the widespread nihilistic element in the intellectual life of our age. Consent to this state of affairs, or that form of consent called indifference, plays its part in *Caligula* and finds expression in the hedonism, the instinctualism or the tragic stoicism of the early collections of essays, *L'Envers et l'endroit* and *Noces*. Hence the balancing of physical affirmation and intellectual negation in such phrases as 'there is no love of life without despair about life' (*L'Envers et l'endroit*) and 'my whole horror of death derives from my anxious appetite for life' (*Noces*). But Camus's fundamental humanity, together with his persistent search for an elusive happiness, led him before long to match indifference with rebellion and consent with refusal. It is the tension between these terms that gives much of its dramatic impetus to *Le Malentendu*. Rebellion and resistance meet defeat in this particular play, but Camus was soon to move beyond this discouragement to a more positive position. In the twenty-five years of his adult life he travelled the road from nihilism to humanism, from a largely self-indulgent paganism to a passionate defence of the claims of justice and human solidarity. Moreover, he did this with great modesty and integrity, avoiding both fashionable posturing and sectarian bias. One of his essays in *L'Été* outlines the task which he set himself and the path which he followed:

> I do not believe firmly enough in reason to subscribe to the idea of progress or some philosophy of history. But at least I believe that men have not ceased to make progress in becoming aware of their own situation. We have not risen above our human condition, but we understand it better. We know that we are the victims of a dilemma; that we must refuse to accept it and do what is necessary to eradicate it. Our task as men is to find some formulas to pacify the great anguish of human kind. We must put together what has been torn apart, make justice a possibility in an obviously unjust world, render happiness meaningful to peoples poisoned by the sufferings of our age.* This is of course a superhuman task, yet one simply calls 'superhuman' those tasks which men take a very long time to accomplish.

On the face of it there seems to be a considerable intellectual difficulty about going beyond the facts of the absurd if one does not explicitly reject them at some point. Camus did not disavow them, though as early as 1939 he had written in *Alger-Républicain* that 'to establish the absurdity of life cannot be an end but only a beginning'. This fact makes the next stage in his thinking both interesting and complex. What seems to have happened is that the circumstances of

* In *Actuelles II* Camus wrote: 'Do you know that over a period of twenty-five years, between 1922 and 1947, 70 million Europeans – men, women and children – have been uprooted, deported and killed?'

war, together with his experience of the Occupation and Resistance in France from 1942 onwards, presented him with a disturbing emotional and intellectual challenge and also provided a clue to the solution of the problem. At the end of *Le Mythe de Sisyphe* the emphases fell on the moral equivalence of all actions and the need to live each passing moment to the full. These are consequences Camus drew from his analysis of the absurd. But in the concrete situation of occupation and resistance such attitudes, while apparently coherent in logic, were not emotionally tenable for a person of his natural humanity and integrity. A personal, hedonistic ethic could not be sustained in circumstances where moral choices and practical decision meant life or death to others (both unknown individuals and close friends and colleagues). At the same time, Camus had thought a great deal about the whole phenomenon of Nazism. He saw that thinkers like Nietzsche could be interpreted – or misrepresented – in a variety of ways and he was convinced that Nazi doctrine, as certainly as his own ideas in *Le Mythe de Sisyphe*, was the child of modern nihilism. This proposition is set out in the *Lettres à un ami allemand* (written between 1943 and 1945) where Camus admits that he agreed, at one stage, with the diagnosis of the absurdity of existence made by various German writers. He shared their sceptical attitude to moral absolutes and could sympathize, at least in an abstract way, with their resolve to escape from the apparent senselessness of life by means of force, hardness, cunning, national self-aggrandisement. In the circumstances of war, however, despite a common starting-point, he found himself on one side of a moral argument (i.e. in the French Resistance) while the Nazis took their stand on the opposing side. Camus finds the explanation of this situation in one important fact apparently overlooked by German nihilism. The very acceptance of nihilism logically implies the placing of particular value on human life, not an ignoring of it. It implies human solidarity – indeed it contains the seeds of humanism in the most fruitful sense of the term – because since man is 'the one creature whose desire [for value and meaning] is constantly thwarted in the world' it follows that 'man himself possesses value and meaning'. I think this assertion is open to logical objections simply as it stands, but the actual context makes it clear that Camus is claiming that man must have meaning, not perhaps objectively or absolutely, but *for other men.* Three separate lines of argument have therefore led to this position. Firstly, a purely selfish, quantitative ethic proves inadequate in the face of human suffering and human need (the Resistance). Secondly, an abstract interpretation of the absurd can lead to terrible human disasters (Nazi ideology). Thirdly, a closer scrutiny of the absurd shows that some standard of coherence alone makes this concept meaningful. This idea of coherence is something essentially human and concrete. It is the one foothold to be gained on the precipitous face of nihilism and it provides a starting-point for Camus's exploration of a possible route through nihilism to positive humanism.

Because Camus charted the main features of present-day nihilism with clarity and understanding his attempt to fashion what he called 'an art of living in times of catastrophe' was much more persuasive to his contemporaries than it would otherwise have been. The fact that he accepted the worst before attempting to outline some positive reaction to it increased his readers' respect. He confirmed or made articulate many of their own feelings: their sense of the failure of nineteenth-century humanist assumptions; their suspicion of such great rallying words as 'freedom', 'justice', 'honour', 'discipline'; their awareness of the thorough breakdown of so much religious and political idealism. As a result, many were disposed to see him not only as a spokesman but, once he began to reject nihilism, as a potential guide. Camus himself denied any desire to play such a role. His modesty and sense of the depth and complexity of our contemporary *malaise* made him resist any aspirations of this kind. In fact, when he rejects nihilism and moves from 'the doctrine of the absurd' to 'the doctrine of revolt', he has little to offer in the way of detailed, practical advice. The most persuasive aspects of his thought remain negative and analytical rather than positive and prescriptive.

Revolt against the absurd and a positive reaction to nihilism are the main subjects of *L'Homme révolté*. What Camus is looking for here is a strict humanism – strict in the sense that it rejects any form of rebellion involving the idea of transcendence. He regards the religious forms of transcendence – faith in an eternity spent with God – as a desperate leap into irrationality. Put in another way, he sees religious faith as a major attempt to negate the absurd yet one which can only do so by denying that same limited human reason which revealed and affirmed the absurd in the first place. In our own century, however, religious transcendence has been widely replaced by secular counterparts, particularly the Marxist belief in historical inevitability which he terms 'the only transcendence of men without God'. This deification of history he shows to have led to intellectual abstraction of the worst kind. It leads to what Yeats called 'the thoughts men think in the mind alone' – ideas that lack all human warmth and eventually exploit individuals rather than serve them. Hence the attacks on the revolutionary theory and practice of communism in *L'Homme révolté*. Hence, also, Camus's careful distinction between political revolution and his own particular conception of rebellion.

This idea of rebellion is obviously both non-Christian and non-Marxist. It emphasizes nature rather than history, moderation rather than extremism, human concern rather than abstract ideology, the dialogue rather than the directive. A genuine humanism – one which refuses to bend human nature to the demands of an *a priori* intellectual framework – presides over all these attitudes. Camus, the Algerian, locates them in a humane, Mediterranean tradition which is in marked contrast to our 'nordic dreams' of intemperance. It is no doubt obvious that the guide in Camus, as distinct from the spokesman, is vague about details and sometimes has recourse to a lyrical, personal language that uses such terms as *pensée solaire* and *esprit méditerranéen.* Nevertheless, he brought much benefit to his contemporaries by locating and exploring the major problems of his age. The kind of exploration which he carried out, with its emphasis on the needs of individual men and its exposure of murderous ideologies, is an essential step towards any ultimate solution of these problems. The writings on rebellion offer us the only kind of humanism we should ask for – a humanism at once honest in its temper, modest in its claims, and as free from illusions as one man could make it. It is an attempt to point to some possible justification for Unamuno's claim, in *The Tragic Sense of Life*, that 'uncertainty and doubt, perpetual wrestling with the mystery of our fatal destiny, mental despair and the lack of any solid and stable dogmatic foundation, may be the basis of an ethic'.

*

It is not my purpose to discuss in any great detail the two plays that follow. Readers will make their own judgements of them on the basis of the texts printed here. Nevertheless, a few general, explanatory comments may be useful. It is clear that Camus, in common with a number of his French contemporaries, used the theatre primarily as a medium for the expression of serious ideas – moral dilemmas and speculative inquiries of the type outlined above. There are various reasons for this quite widespread tendency in the recent French theatre, a tendency which distinguishes it broadly from its English counterpart. The main reason, however, has to do with the philosophical presuppositions of dramatists such as Sartre, Simone de Beauvoir, Marcel, and Camus. Whatever their differences, all of them have in common a conviction that moral and philosophical dilemmas must be approached from a concrete, human standpoint – as a living individual might encounter them. The result is that they find the theatre, in so far as it works through individuals towards ideas, a natural vehicle of expression. Yet because of the abstract ideas which dominate their thinking about individuals, these dramatists present plays which are broadly situational rather than analytical on the psychological level. To this extent characters are not portrayed mainly for their intrinsic interest as individuals but because they can act out certain moral problems of mankind at large. It is this intention to explore aspects of 'the human condition' that requires Anglo-Saxon audiences to make some effort of adjustment before judging such plays as *Caligula* and *Cross Purpose*.

Both plays belong to the earlier, predominantly negative and nihilistic, phase of Camus's thought. In the case of *Caligula*, and in keeping with the point just made above, Camus's aim is not to study the psychology of a monster in human form but to investigate the consequences of taking a nihilistic response to the absurd to its apparently logical conclusions. In so far as this is precisely what Camus claimed that Nazi doctrine did, the play – even in its original form of 1938 – is a strange and striking anticipation, in the person of Caligula himself, of those 'mad emperors' who derived their political logic from nihilism between 1939 and 1945.

Originally written in 1938, the play was re-worked to some extent both in 1945 and in 1958, though the first version underwent no fundamental alteration. Camus drew his material directly from Suetonius' *Lives of the Twelve Caesars* and claimed to have followed the Latin historian faithfully. He naturally interprets the original material in accordance with his own ideas, but he invented none of the main scenes such as the worship of Caligula dressed as Venus and the 'poetic contest' on the theme of death. We also find in Suetonius accounts of Caligula's scheme to contrive a famine and his plan to open brothels as a source of private income, while there are references to his restlessness and insomnia, his apparent madness, his grimacing in front of the mirror, and his wooing of the moon. The strict historical facts appear to be that Caius Caesar Caligula, third of the twelve Caesars, came to power in A.D. 37 at the age of twenty-five and reigned for four years until his assassination in A.D. 41. For the first eight months of his reign he proved a relatively enlightened and generous ruler, but about this time he conceived an incestuous love for his sister Drusilla and announced his intention of marrying her. Drusilla suddenly died, however, and Caligula's character apparently changed completely so that Suetonius speaks of him as having become 'rather a monster than a man'. He killed or tortured many of his subjects so that the patricians finally came out in open rebellion and assassinated him.

The one point at which Camus gives us a distinctly personal gloss on Caligula's behaviour is his explanation of the emperor's abrupt reversal of character and apparent madness after Drusilla's death. Suetonius speaks of epilepsy or a philtre given to Caligula by Caesonia which had the effect of driving him mad. Camus, however, treats Drusilla's death as an experience which suddenly reveals the nature of the absurd to Caligula and the truth that 'men die and are not happy'. It is this feature of our human condition which Caligula presses to what he considers its logical conclusion. He does so in the belief that such an action can confer freedom upon him, yet in the course of the play he learns that one cannot be free *against* others. Camus's own explanation of the play's meaning is contained in a note included in the programme for the Hébertot production:

> . . . if his integrity consists in his denial of the gods, his fault is to be found in his denial of men. One cannot destroy everything without destroying oneself. This is why Caligula depopulates the world around him and then, in keeping with his own logic, does what is necessary to arm against himself those who will ultimately kill him. Caligula's story is that of a high-minded type of suicide. It is an account of the most human and most tragic of mistakes. Caligula is faithless towards humanity in order to keep faith with himself. He consents to die, having learned that no man can save himself alone and that one cannot be free by working against mankind. But at least he will have rescued some souls, including his own and that of his friend Scipio, from the dreamless sleep of mediocrity.

The sombre material of *Cross Purpose* is briefly mentioned in the second part of Camus's novel, *L'Étranger*. Meursault finds a yellowed piece of newspaper sticking to the underside of the mattress in his prison cell. This scrap of paper reports the story of a man who returned to his native Czechoslovakia after many years abroad and stayed at an inn run by his mother and sister without revealing his identity to them. Only after they have murdered him for gain – as they had done with previous guests – do the mother and sister realize the exact nature of their crime. Having done so, both commit suicide. Meursault's comment is that in one way he finds the story improbable yet in another quite natural. He adds that the son was guilty in so far as 'one should never fool around'.

This *fait-divers* naturally provides the basis for a deeply pessimistic play. In *Caligula* Camus portrayed what he considered to be one individual's deeply mistaken reaction to his discovery of the absurd. In *Cross Purpose*, on the other hand, it is the injustice and misunderstanding built into the world as we know it – the absurd fabric of existence itself – that frustrates and confounds individuals rendered powerless before it. In this aspect at least, *Cross Purpose* is much the more pessimistic of the two plays. It emphasizes human experience of the absurd by stressing the failure of human beings to communicate adequately, the obstacles lying in the path of a direct and simple desire for happiness, the sense of solitude or exile which affects the main characters. Jan seeks happiness through integration, solidarity, spontaneous recognition. Martha wants to escape to the sea and the sunlight and plans to use the money stolen from murdered guests for this purpose. Both reactions meet inevitable failure in a universe where inexplicable, arbitrary, cruel things happen alike to those who have chosen crime and those who have chosen innocence. Ironically too, what seem like morally regenerative actions can seal and confirm an individual's 'condemnation'. Thus when Jan manages to appeal to the small human residue in Martha's almost inhumanly harsh nature he makes his own death inevitable. Martha explains that when he evoked a response from her by speaking of the sun-drenched country of which she had always dreamt he provided her with weapons against himself. He unwittingly renewed her reasons for killing him and she says bitterly: 'That is how innocence is rewarded.'

The absurdity or incoherence of life is not merely implicit in the subject matter of *Cross Purpose*. It is directly referred to in the text on a number of occasions. In the third act, for example, the mother speaks of 'this earth where nothing's sure' and asserts that 'this world we live in doesn't make sense'. Similarly Martha says to the wife of the brother she has murdered:

neither for him nor for us, neither in life nor in death, is there any peace or homeland. For you'll agree one can hardly call it a home, that place of clotted darkness underground, to which we go from here, to feed blind animals.

Hence her final piece of advice to Maria:

Pray your God to harden you to stone. It's the happiness He has assigned Himself, and the one true happiness. Do as He does, be deaf to all appeals, and turn your heart to stone while there still is time.

This seems to be the final, despairing message of the play, yet Camus was reported as saying, as early as 1944, that this apparent pessimism hid a deeper optimism in the sense that 'man, freed from his illusions and his gods, can find in action and revolt the only liberty which he can bear'. Such a comment as this, even if it can be justified by a performance or a reading of the play itself, leans rather heavily on a positive interpretation of Jan's negative behaviour. Camus revealed this himself when he stated shortly afterwards:

Finally it comes down to saying that everything would have been different if the son had said: 'It's me, this is my name.' It comes down to saying that in an unjust and indifferent world, man can still achieve his own salvation and that of other people by the use of the simplest sincerity and the most precise language.

This, in very concentrated form, is indeed the position towards which Camus was working at the time in his transition from the doctrine of the absurd to the doctrine of rebellion. However, it is not, in my view, the real burden of the play. Indeed, it relies for acceptance on a situation which would make it impossible for the play to be written. The last suggestion that *Cross Purpose* makes is that human action can really change anything, and it is in its exploration of this point of view that its real interest lies. In fact these two plays, *Caligula* and *Cross Purpose*, belong entirely to the most negative period of Camus's thought. Together, they chart the main features of the absurd. Individually, *Caligula* describes a mistaken 'solution' while *Cross Purpose* suggests that no solution seems possible. It is in quite different, later plays and novels that Camus draws the outlines of what he considers the right solution to be.

JOHN CRUICKSHANK

CALIGULA

A Play in Four Acts

Characters

CALIGULA, *aged from twenty-five to twenty-nine*
CAESONIA, *Caligula's mistress, aged thirty*
HELICON, *Caligula's intimate friend, aged thirty*
SCIPIO, *aged seventeen*
CHEREA, *aged thirty*
THE OLD PATRICIAN, *aged seventy-one*
MEREIA, *aged sixty*
MUCIUS, *aged thirty-three*
THE INTENDANT, *aged fifty*
FIRST PATRICIAN, SECOND PATRICIAN, THIRD PATRICIAN } *aged from forty to sixty*
KNIGHTS, PALACE GUARDS, SERVANTS

The scene of the First, Third and Fourth Acts is a State Room in the Imperial Palace. In it are a mirror (man's height), a gong, and a couch. The scene of the Second Act is CHEREA's dining-room.

ACT ONE

A number of PATRICIANS, *one a very old man, are gathered in a State Room of the Palace. They are showing signs of nervousness.*

FIRST PATRICIAN: Still no news.

THE OLD PATRICIAN: None last night, none this morning.

SECOND PATRICIAN: Three days without news. Strange indeed!

THE OLD PATRICIAN: Our messengers go out, our messengers return. And always they shake their heads and say, 'Nothing'.

SECOND PATRICIAN: They've combed the whole countryside. What more can be done?

FIRST PATRICIAN: We can only wait. It's no use meeting trouble half way. Perhaps he'll return as abruptly as he left us.

THE OLD PATRICIAN: When I saw him leaving the Palace, I noticed a queer look in his eyes.

FIRST PATRICIAN: Yes, so did I. In fact I asked him what was amiss.

SECOND PATRICIAN: Did he answer?

FIRST PATRICIAN: One word. 'Nothing.'

[*A short silence.* HELICON *enters. He is munching onions.*]

SECOND PATRICIAN [*in the same nervous tone*]: It's all very perturbing.

FIRST PATRICIAN: Oh, come now! All young fellows are like that.

THE OLD PATRICIAN: You're right there. They take things hard. But time smooths everything out.

SECOND PATRICIAN: Do you really think so?

THE OLD PATRICIAN: Of course. For one girl dead, a dozen living ones.

HELICON: Ah? So you think that there's a girl behind it?

FIRST PATRICIAN: What else should there be? Anyhow – thank goodness! – grief never lasts for ever. Is any one of us here capable of mourning a loss for more than a year on end?

SECOND PATRICIAN: Not I, anyhow.

FIRST PATRICIAN: No one can do that.

THE OLD PATRICIAN: Life would be intolerable if one could.

FIRST PATRICIAN: Quite so. Take my case. I lost my wife last year. I shed many tears, and then I forgot. Even now I feel a pang of grief at times. But, happily, it doesn't amount to much.

THE OLD PATRICIAN: Yes, Nature's a great healer.

[CHEREA *enters.*]

FIRST PATRICIAN: Well . . . ?

CHEREA: Still nothing.

HELICON: Come, gentlemen! There's no need for consternation.

FIRST PATRICIAN: I agree.

HELICON: Worrying won't mend matters – and it's lunch-time.

THE OLD PATRICIAN: That's so. We mustn't drop the prey for the shadow.

CHEREA: I don't like the look of things. But all was going too smoothly. As an emperor, he was perfection's self.

SECOND PATRICIAN: Yes, exactly the emperor we wanted; conscientious and inexperienced.

FIRST PATRICIAN: But what's come over you? There's no reason for all these lamentations. We've no ground for assuming he will change. Let's say he loved Drusilla. Only natural; she was his sister. Or say his love for her was something more than brotherly; shocking enough, I grant you. But it's really going too far, setting all Rome in a turmoil because the girl has died.

CHEREA: Maybe. But, as I said, I don't like the look of things; this escapade alarms me.

THE OLD PATRICIAN: Yes, there's never smoke without fire.

FIRST PATRICIAN: In any case, the interests of the State should prevent his making a public tragedy of . . . of, let's say, a regrettable attachment. No doubt such things happen; but the less said the better.

HELICON: How can you be sure Drusilla is the cause of all this trouble?

SECOND PATRICIAN: Who else should it be?

HELICON: Nobody at all, quite likely. When there's a host of explanations to choose from, why pick on the stupidest, most obvious one?

[*Young* SCIPIO *enters.* CHEREA *goes towards him.*]

CHEREA: Well?

SCIPIO: Still nothing. Except that some peasants think they saw him last night not far from Rome, rushing through the storm.

[CHEREA *comes back to the Patricians,* SCIPIO *following him.*]

CHEREA: That makes three days, Scipio, doesn't it?

SCIPIO: Yes . . . I was there, following him as I usually do. He went up to Drusilla's body. He stroked it with two fingers, and seemed lost in thought for a long while. Then he swung round and walked out, calmly enough. . . . And ever since we've been hunting for him – in vain.

CHEREA [*shaking his head*]: That young man was too fond of literature.

SECOND PATRICIAN: Oh, at his age, you know . . .

CHEREA: At his age, perhaps; but not in his position. An

artistic emperor is an anomaly. I grant you we've had one or two; misfits happen in the best of empires. But the others had the good taste to remember they were public servants.

FIRST PATRICIAN: It made things run more smoothly.

THE OLD PATRICIAN: One man, one job – that's how it should be.

SCIPIO: What can we do, Cherea?

CHEREA: Nothing.

SECOND PATRICIAN: We can only wait. If he doesn't return, a successor will have to be found. Between ourselves – there's no shortage of candidates.

FIRST PATRICIAN: No, but there's a shortage of the right sort.

CHEREA: Suppose he comes back in an ugly mood?

FIRST PATRICIAN: Oh, he's a mere boy; we'll make him see reason.

CHEREA: And what if he declines to see it?

FIRST PATRICIAN [*laughing*]: In that case, my friend, don't forget I once wrote a manual of revolutions. You'll find all the rules there.

CHEREA: I'll look it up – if things come to that. But I'd rather be left to my books.

SCIPIO: If you'll excuse me ... [*Goes out.*]

CHEREA: He's huffed.

THE OLD PATRICIAN: Scipio is young, and young folk always hang together.

HELICON: Scipio doesn't count, anyhow.

[*Enter a member of the Imperial Bodyguard.*]

THE GUARDSMAN: Caligula has been seen in the Palace Gardens.

[*All leave the room. The stage is empty for some moments. Then* CALIGULA *enters stealthily from the left. His legs are caked with mud, his garments dirty; his hair is wet, his look dis-*

traught. He brings his hand to his mouth several times. Then he approaches a mirror, stopping abruptly when he catches sight of his reflected self. After muttering some unintelligible words, he sits down on the right, letting his arms hang limp between his knees. HELICON *enters, left. On seeing Caligula, he stops at the far end of the stage and contemplates him in silence.* CALIGULA *turns and sees him. A short silence.*

HELICON [*across the stage*]: Good morning, Caius.

CALIGULA [*in quite an ordinary tone*]: Good morning, Helicon.

[*A short silence.*]

HELICON: You're looking tired.

CALIGULA: I've walked a lot.

HELICON: Yes, you've been away for quite a while.

[*Another short silence.*]

CALIGULA: It was hard to find.

HELICON: What was hard to find?

CALIGULA: What I was after.

HELICON: Meaning?

CALIGULA [*in the same matter-of-fact tone*]: The moon.

HELICON: What?

CALIGULA: Yes, I wanted the moon.

HELICON: Ah . . . [*Another silence.* HELICON *approaches Caligula.*] And why did you want it?

CALIGULA: Well . . . it's one of the things I haven't got.

HELICON: I see. And now – have you fixed it up to your satisfaction?

CALIGULA: No. I couldn't get it.

HELICON: Too bad!

CALIGULA: Yes, and that's why I'm tired. [*Pauses. Then*] Helicon!

HELICON: Yes, Caius?

CALIGULA: No doubt, you think I'm crazy.

HELICON: As you know well, I never think.

CALIGULA: Ah yes . . . Now, listen! I'm not mad; in fact

I've never felt so lucid. What happened to me is quite simple; I suddenly felt a desire for the impossible. That's all. [*Pauses.*] Things as they are, in my opinion, are far from satisfactory.

HELICON: Many people share your opinion.

CALIGULA: That is so. But in the past I didn't realize it. *Now* I know. [*Still in the same matter-of-fact tone*] Really, this world of ours, the scheme of things as they call it, is quite intolerable. That's why I want the moon, or happiness, or eternal life – something, in fact, that may sound crazy, but which isn't of this world.

HELICON: That's sound enough in theory. Only, in practice one can't carry it through to its conclusion.

CALIGULA [*rising to his feet, but still with perfect calmness*]: You're wrong there. It's just because no one *dares* to follow up his ideas to the end that nothing is achieved. All that's needed, I should say, is to be logical right through, at all costs. [*He studies Helicon's face.*] I can see, too, what you're thinking. What a pother over a woman's death! But that's not it. True enough, I seem to remember that a woman died some days ago; a woman whom I loved. But love, what is it? A side-issue. And I swear to you her death is not the point; it's no more than the symbol of a truth that makes the moon essential to me. A childishly simple, obvious, almost silly truth, but one that's hard to come by and heavy to endure.

HELICON: May I know what it is, this truth that you've discovered?

CALIGULA [*his eyes averted, in a toneless voice*]: Men die; and they are not happy.

HELICON [*after a short pause*]: Anyhow, Caligula, it's a truth with which one comes to terms, without much trouble. Only look at the people over there. This truth of yours doesn't prevent them from enjoying their meal.

CALIGULA [*with sudden violence*]: All it proves is that I'm surrounded by lies and self-deception. But I've had enough of that; I wish men to live by the light of truth. And I've the power to make them do so. For I know what they need and haven't got. They're without understanding and they need a teacher; someone who knows what he's talking about.

HELICON: Don't take offence, Caius, if I give you a word of advice . . . But that can wait. First, you should have some rest.

CALIGULA [*sitting down. His voice is gentle again*]: That's not possible, Helicon. I shall never rest again.

HELICON: But – why?

CALIGULA: If I sleep, who'll give me the moon?

HELICON [*after a short silence*]: That's true.

CALIGULA [*rising to his feet again, with an effort*]: Listen, Helicon . . . I hear footsteps, voices. Say nothing – and forget you've seen me.

HELICON: I understand.

CALIGULA [*looking back, as he moves towards the door*]: And please help me, from now on.

HELICON: I've no reason not to do so, Caius. But I know very few things, and few things interest me. In what way can I help you?

CALIGULA: In the way of . . . the impossible.

HELICON: I'll do my best.

[CALIGULA *goes out.* SCIPIO *and* CAESONIA *enter hurriedly.*]

SCIPIO: No one! Haven't you seen him?

HELICON: No.

CAESONIA: Tell me, Helicon. Are you quite sure he didn't say anything to you before he went away?

HELICON: I'm not a sharer of his secrets, I'm his public. A mere onlooker. It's more prudent.

CAESONIA: Please don't talk like that.

HELICON: My dear Caesonia, Caius is an idealist as we all know. He follows his bent, and no one can foresee where it will take him . . . But, if you'll excuse me, I'll go to lunch. [*Exit.*]

CAESONIA [*sinking wearily on to a divan*]: One of the Palace Guards saw him go by. But all Rome sees Caligula everywhere. And Caligula, of course, sees nothing but his own idea.

SCIPIO: What idea?

CAESONIA: How can I tell, Scipio?

SCIPIO: Are you thinking of Drusilla?

CAESONIA: Perhaps. One thing is sure; he loved her. And it's a cruel thing to have someone die today whom only yesterday you were holding in your arms.

SCIPIO [*timidly*]: And you . . . ?

CAESONIA: Oh, I'm the old, trusted mistress. That's my role.

SCIPIO: Caesonia, we must save him.

CAESONIA: So you, too, love him?

SCIPIO: Yes. He's been very good to me. He encouraged me; I shall never forget some of the things he said. He told me life isn't easy, but it has consolations: religion, art, and the love one inspires in others. He often told me that the only mistake one makes in life is to cause others suffering. He tried to be a just man.

CAESONIA [*rising*]: He's only a child. [*She goes to the glass and scans herself.*] The only god I've ever had is my body, and now I shall pray this god of mine to give Caius back to me.

[CALIGULA *enters. On seeing Caesonia and Scipio he hesitates, and takes a backward step. At the same moment several men enter from the opposite side of the room:* PATRICIANS *and the* INTENDANT *of the Palace. They stop short when they see Caligula.* CAESONIA *turns. She and* SCIPIO *hurry towards Caligula, who checks them with a gesture.*

INTENDANT [*in a rather quavering voice*]: We . . . we've been looking for you, Caesar, high and low.

CALIGULA [*in a changed, harsh tone*]: So I see.

INTENDANT: We . . . I mean . . .

CALIGULA [*roughly*]: What do you want?

INTENDANT: We were feeling anxious, Caesar.

CALIGULA [*going towards him*]: What business had you to feel anxious?

INTENDANT: Well . . . er . . . [*He has an inspiration.*] Well, as you know, there are points to be settled in connexion with the Treasury.

CALIGULA [*bursting into laughter*]: Ah, yes. The Treasury! That's so. The Treasury's of prime importance.

INTENDANT: Yes, indeed.

CALIGULA [*still laughing, to Caesonia*]: Don't you agree, my dear? The Treasury is all-important.

CAESONIA: No, Caligula. It's a secondary matter.

CALIGULA: That only shows your ignorance. We are extremely interested in our Treasury. Everything's important: our fiscal system, public morals, foreign policy, army equipment, and agrarian laws. Everything's of cardinal importance, I assure you. And everything's on an equal footing: the grandeur of Rome and your attacks of arthritis. . . . Well, well, I'm going to apply my mind to all that. And, to begin with . . . Now listen well, Intendant.

INTENDANT: We are listening, sir.

[*The* PATRICIANS *come forward.*]

CALIGULA: You're our loyal subjects, are you not?

INTENDANT [*in a reproachful tone*]: Oh, Caesar! . . .

CALIGULA: Well, I've something to propose to you. We're going to make a complete change in our economic system. In two moves. Drastic and abrupt. I'll explain, Intendant . . . when the Patricians have left. [*The*

PATRICIANS *go out.* CALIGULA *seats himself beside Caesonia, with his arm round her waist.*] Now mark my words. The first move's this. Every Patrician, everyone in the Empire who has any capital – small or large, it's all the same thing – is ordered to disinherit his children and make a new will leaving his money to the State.

INTENDANT: But Caesar . . .

CALIGULA: I've not yet given you leave to speak. As the need arises, we shall have these people die; a list will be drawn up by us fixing the order of their deaths. When the fancy takes us, we may modify that order. And, of course, we shall step into their money.

CAESONIA [*freeing herself*]: But – what's come over you?

CALIGULA [*imperturbably*]: Obviously the order of their going has no importance. Or, rather, all these executions have an equal importance – from which it follows that none has any. Really all those fellows are on a par, one's as guilty as another. [*To the Intendant, peremptorily*] You are to promulgate this edict without a moment's delay and see it's carried out forthwith. The wills are to be signed by residents in Rome this evening; within a month at the latest by persons in the provinces. Send out your messengers.

INTENDANT: Caesar, I wonder if you realize . . .

CALIGULA: Do I realize . . . ? Now, listen well, you fool! If the Treasury has paramount importance, human life has none. That should be obvious to you. People who think like you are bound to admit the logic of my edict and, since money is the only thing that counts, should set no value on their lives or anyone else's. I have resolved to be logical, and I have the power to enforce my will. Presently you'll see what logic's going to cost you; I shall eliminate contradictions and contradictors. If necessary, I'll begin with you.

INTENDANT: Caesar, my good will can be relied on, that I swear.

CALIGULA: And mine, too; that I guarantee. Just see how ready I am to adopt your point of view, and give the Treasury the first place in my programme. Really you should be grateful to me; I'm playing into your hand, and with your own cards. [*He pauses, before continuing in a flat, unemotional tone.*] In any case there is a touch of genius in the simplicity of my plan – which clinches the matter. I give you three seconds in which to remove yourself. One . . .

[*The* INTENDANT *hurries out.*]

CAESONIA: I can't believe it's you! But it was just a joke, wasn't it? – all you said to him.

CALIGULA: Not quite that, Caesonia. Let's say, a lesson in statesmanship.

SCIPIO: But Caius, it's . . . it's impossible!

CALIGULA: That's the whole point.

SCIPIO: I don't follow.

CALIGULA: I repeat – that is my point. I'm exploiting the impossible. Or, more accurately, it's a question of making the impossible possible.

SCIPIO: But that game may lead to – to anything! It's a lunatic's pastime.

CALIGULA: No, Scipio. An emperor's vocation. [*He lets himself sink back wearily amongst the cushions.*] Ah, my dears, at last I've come to see the uses of supremacy. It gives impossibilities a run. From this day on, so long as life is mine, my freedom has no frontier.

CAESONIA [*sadly*]: I doubt if this discovery of yours will make us any happier.

CALIGULA: So do I. But, I suppose, we'll have to live it through.

[CHEREA *enters.*]

CHEREA: I have just heard of your return. I trust your health is all it should be.

CALIGULA: My health is duly grateful. [*A pause. Then, abruptly*] Leave us, Cherea. I don't want to see you.

CHEREA: Really, Caius, I'm amazed . . .

CALIGULA: There's nothing to be amazed at. I don't like literary men, and I can't bear lies.

CHEREA: If we lie, it's often without knowing it. I plead Not Guilty.

CALIGULA: Lies are never guiltless. And yours attribute importance to people and to things. That's what I cannot forgive you.

CHEREA: And yet – since this world is the only one we have, why not plead its cause?

CALIGULA: Your pleading comes too late, the verdict's given . . . This world has no importance; once a man realizes that, he wins his freedom. [*He has risen to his feet.*] And that is why I hate you, you and your kind; because you are not free. You see in me the one free man in the whole Roman Empire. You should be glad to have at last amongst you an emperor who points the way to freedom. Leave me, Cherea; and you, too, Scipio, go – for what is friendship? Go, both of you, and spread the news in Rome that freedom has been given her at last, and with the gift begins a great probation.

[*They go out.* CALIGULA *has turned away, hiding his eyes.*]

CAESONIA: Crying?

CALIGULA: Yes, Caesonia.

CAESONIA: But, after all, what's changed in your life? You may have loved Drusilla, but you loved many others – myself included – at the same time. Surely that wasn't enough to set you roaming the countryside for three days and nights and bring you back with this . . . this cruel look on your face?

CALIGULA [*swinging round on her*]: What nonsense is this? Why drag in Drusilla? Do you imagine love's the only thing that can make a man shed tears?

CAESONIA: I'm sorry, Caius. Only I was trying to understand.

CALIGULA: Men weep because . . . the world's all wrong.

[*She comes towards him.*]

CALIGULA: No, Caesonia.

[*She draws back.*]

CALIGULA: But stay beside me.

CAESONIA: I'll do whatever you wish. [*Sits down.*] At my age one knows that life's a sad business. But why deliberately set out to make it worse?

CALIGULA: No it's no good; you can't understand. But what matter? Perhaps I'll find a way out. Only, I feel a curious stirring within me, as if undreamt-of things were forcing their way up into the light – and I'm helpless against them. [*He moves closer to her.*] Oh, Caesonia, I knew that men felt anguish, but I didn't know what that word, anguish, meant. Like everyone else I fancied it was a sickness of the mind – no more. But no, it's my body that's in pain. Pain everywhere, in my chest, in my legs and arms. Even my skin is raw, my head is buzzing, I feel like vomiting. But worst of all is this queer taste in my mouth. Not blood, or death, or fever, but a mixture of all three. I've only to stir my tongue, and the world goes black, and everyone looks . . . horrible. How hard, how cruel it is, this process of becoming a man!

CAESONIA: What you need, my dear, is a good, long sleep. Let yourself relax and, above all, stop thinking. I'll stay by you while you sleep. And when you wake, you'll find the world's got back its savour. Then you must use your power to good effect – for loving better what you still find lovable. For the possible, too, deserves to be given a chance.

CALIGULA: Ah, but for that I'd need to sleep, to let myself go – and that's impossible.

CAESONIA: So one always thinks when one is over-tired. A time comes when one's hand is firm again.

CALIGULA: But one must know where to place it. And what's the use to me of a firm hand, what use is the amazing power that's mine, if I can't have the sun set in the east, if I can't reduce the sum of suffering and make an end of death? No, Caesonia, it's all one whether I sleep or keep awake, if I've no power to tamper with the scheme of things.

CAESONIA: But that's madness, sheer madness. It's wanting to be a god on earth.

CALIGULA: So you, too, think I'm mad. And yet – what is a god that I should wish to be his equal? No, it's something higher, far above the gods, that I'm aiming at, longing for with all my heart and soul. I am taking over a kingdom where the impossible is king.

CAESONIA: You can't prevent the sky from being the sky, or a fresh young face from ageing, or a man's heart from growing cold.

CALIGULA [*with rising excitement*]: I want . . . I want to drown the sky in the sea, to infuse ugliness with beauty, to wring a laugh from pain.

CAESONIA [*facing him with an imploring gesture*]: There's good and bad, high and low, justice and injustice. And I swear to you these will never change.

CALIGULA [*in the same tone*]: And I'm resolved to change them . . . I shall make this age of ours a kingly gift – the gift of equality. And when all is levelled out, when the impossible has come to earth and the moon is in my hands – then, perhaps, I shall be transfigured and the world renewed; then men will die no more and at last be happy.

CAESONIA [*with a little cry*]: And love? Surely you won't go back on love!

CALIGULA [*in a wild burst of anger*]: Love, Caesonia! [*He grips her shoulders and shakes her.*] I've learnt the truth about love; it's nothing, nothing! That fellow was quite right – you heard what he said, didn't you? – it's only the Treasury that counts. The fountain-head of all. Ah, now at last I'm going to live, really *live*. And living, my dear, is the opposite of loving. I know what I'm talking about – and I invite you to the most gorgeous of shows, a sight for gods to gloat on, a whole world called to judgement. But for that I must have a crowd – spectators, victims, criminals, hundreds and thousands of them. [*He rushes to the gong and begins hammering on it, faster and faster.*] Let the accused come forward. I want my criminals, and they all are criminals. [*Still striking the gong*] Bring in the condemned men. I must have my public. Judges, witnesses, accused – all sentenced to death without a hearing. Yes, Caesonia, I'll show them something they have never seen before, the one free man in the Roman Empire.

[*To the clangour of the gong the Palace has been gradually filling with noises; the clash of arms, voices, footsteps slow or hurried, coming nearer, growing louder. Some soldiers enter, and leave hastily.*]

CALIGULA: And you, Caesonia, shall obey me. You must stand by me to the end. It will be marvellous, you'll see. Swear to stand by me, Caesonia.

CAESONIA [*wildly, between two gong-strokes*]: I needn't swear. You know I love you.

CALIGULA [*in the same tone*]: You'll do all I tell you.

CAESONIA: All, all, Caligula – but do, please, stop . . .

CALIGULA [*still striking the gong*]: You will be cruel.

CAESONIA [*sobbing*]: Cruel.

CALIGULA [*still beating the gong*]: Cold and ruthless.

CAESONIA: Ruthless.

CALIGULA: And you will suffer, too.

CAESONIA: Yes, yes – oh, no, please . . . I'm – I'm going mad, I think!

[*Some* PATRICIANS *enter, followed by members of the Palace staff. All look bewildered and perturbed.* CALIGULA *bangs the gong for the last time, raises his mallet, swings round, and summons them in a shrill, half-crazy voice.*]

CALIGULA: Come here. All of you. Nearer. Nearer still. [*He is quivering with impatience.*] Your Emperor commands you to come nearer.

[*They come forward, pale with terror.*]

CALIGULA: Quickly. And you, Caesonia, come beside me. [*He takes her hand, leads her to the mirror and with a wild sweep of his mallet effaces a reflection on its surface. Then gives a sudden laugh.*] All gone. You see, my dear? An end of memories; no more masks. Nothing, nobody left. Nobody? No, that's not true. Look, Caesonia. Come here, all of you, and *look* . . . [*He plants himself in front of the mirror in a grotesque attitude.*]

CAESONIA [*staring, horrified, at the mirror*]: Caligula!

[CALIGULA *lays a finger on the glass. His gaze steadies abruptly and when he speaks his voice has a new, proud ardour.*]

CALIGULA: Yes . . . Caligula.

CURTAIN

ACT TWO

A room in Cherea's house where the Patricians have met in secret.

FIRST PATRICIAN: It's outrageous, the way he's treating us.

THE OLD PATRICIAN: He calls me 'darling'! In public, mind you – just to make a laughing-stock of me. Death's too good for him.

FIRST PATRICIAN: And fancy making us run beside his litter when he goes into the country.

SECOND PATRICIAN: He says the exercise will do us good.

THE OLD PATRICIAN: Conduct like that is quite inexcusable.

THIRD PATRICIAN: You're right. That's precisely the sort of thing one can't forgive.

FIRST PATRICIAN: He confiscated your property, Patricius. He killed your father, Scipio. He's taken your wife from you, Octavius, and forced her to work in his public brothel. He has killed your son, Lepidus. I ask you, gentlemen, can you endure this? I, anyhow, have made my mind up. I know the risks, but I also know this life of abject fear is quite unbearable. Worse than death, in fact. Yes, as I said, my mind's made up.

SCIPIO: He made my mind up for me when he had my father put to death.

FIRST PATRICIAN: Well? Can you still hesitate?

A KNIGHT: No. We're with you. He's transferred our stalls at the Circus to the public, and egged us on to fight with the rabble – just to have a pretext for punishing us, of course.

THE OLD PATRICIAN: He's a coward.

SECOND PATRICIAN: A bully.

THIRD PATRICIAN: A buffoon.

THE OLD PATRICIAN: He's impotent – that's his trouble, I should say.

[*A scene of wild confusion follows, weapons are brandished, a table is overturned, and there is a general rush towards the door. Just at this moment* CHEREA *strolls in, composed as usual, and checks their onrush.*]

CHEREA: What's all this about? Where are you going?

A PATRICIAN: To the Palace.

CHEREA: Ah, yes. And I can guess why. But do you think you'll be allowed to enter?

THE PATRICIAN: There's no question of asking leave.

CHEREA: Lepidus, would you kindly shut that door?

[*The door is shut.* CHEREA *goes to the upturned table and seats himself on a corner of it. The others turn towards him.*]

CHEREA: It's not so simple as you think, my friends. You're afraid, but fear can't take the place of courage and deliberation. In short, you're acting too hastily.

A KNIGHT: If you're not with us, go. But keep your mouth shut.

CHEREA: I suspect I'm with you. But make no mistake. Not for the same reasons.

A VOICE: That's enough idle talk.

CHEREA [*standing up*]: I agree. Let's get down to facts. But, first, let me make myself clear. Though I am *with* you, I'm not *for* you. That, indeed, is why I think you're going about it the wrong way. You haven't taken your enemy's measure; that's obvious, since you attribute petty motives to him. But there's nothing petty about Caligula, and you're riding for a fall. You'd be better placed to fight him if you would try to see him as he really is.

A VOICE: We see him as he is – a crazy tyrant.

CHEREA: No. We've had experience of mad emperors. But this one isn't mad enough. And what I loathe in him is this: that he knows what he wants.

FIRST PATRICIAN: And we, too, know it; he wants to murder us all.

CHEREA: You're wrong. Our deaths are only a side-issue. He's putting his power at the service of a loftier, deadlier passion; and it imperils everything we hold most sacred. True, it's not the first time Rome has seen a man wielding unlimited power; but it's the first time he sets no limit to his use of it, and counts mankind, and the world we know, for nothing. That's what appals me in Caligula; that's what I want to fight. To lose one's life is no great matter; when the time comes I'll have the courage to lose mine. But what's intolerable is to see one's life being drained of meaning, to be told there's no reason for existing. A man can't live without some reason for living.

FIRST PATRICIAN: Revenge is a good reason.

CHEREA: Yes, and I propose to share it with you. But I'd have you know that it's not on your account, or to help you to avenge your petty humiliations. No, if I join forces with you, it's to combat a big idea – an ideal, if you like – whose triumph would mean the end of everything. I can endure your being made a mock of, but I cannot endure Caligula's carrying out his theories to the end. He is converting his philosophy into corpses and – unfortunately for us – it's a philosophy that's logical from start to finish. And where one can't refute, one strikes.

A VOICE: Yes. We must *act*.

CHEREA: We must take action, I agree. But a frontal attack's quite useless when one is fighting an imperial madman in the full flush of his power. You can take arms against a vulgar tyrant, but cunning is needed to fight down disinterested malice. You can only urge it on to follow its bent, and bide your time until its logic founders in sheer lunacy. As you see, I prefer to be quite frank, and I warn you I'll be with you only for a time. Afterwards, I shall do nothing to advance your interests; all I wish is to regain some peace of mind in a world that has regained a meaning. What spurs me on is not ambition but fear, my very reasonable fear of that inhuman vision in which my life means no more than a speck of dust.

FIRST PATRICIAN [*approaching him*]: I have an inkling of what you mean, Cherea. Anyhow, the great thing is that you, too, feel that the whole fabric of society is threatened. You, gentlemen, agree with me, I take it, that our ruling motive is of a moral order. Family life is breaking down, men are losing their respect for honest work, a wave of immorality is sweeping the country. Who of us can be deaf to the appeal of our ancestral piety in its hour of danger? Fellow-conspirators, will you tolerate a state of things in which patricians are forced to run, like slaves, beside the Emperor's litter?

THE OLD PATRICIAN: Will you allow them to be addressed as 'darling'?

A VOICE: And have their wives snatched from them?

ANOTHER VOICE: And their money?

ALL TOGETHER: No!

FIRST PATRICIAN: Cherea, your advice is good, and you did well to calm our passion. The time is not yet ripe for action; the masses would still be against us. Will you join us in watching for the best moment to strike – and strike hard?

CHEREA: Yes – and meanwhile let Caligula follow his dream. Or, rather, let's actively encourage him to carry out his wildest plans. Let's put method into his madness. And then, at last, a day will come when he's alone, a lonely man in an empire of the dead and kinsmen of the dead.

[*A general uproar. Trumpet-calls outside. Then silence, but for whispers of a name: 'Caligula!'* CALIGULA *enters with* CAESONIA, *followed by* HELICON *and some soldiers. Dumb-show.* CALIGULA *halts and gazes at the conspirators. Without a word he moves from one to the other, straightens a buckle on one man's shoulder, steps back to contemplate another, sweeps them with his gaze, then draws his hand over his eyes and walks out, still without a word.*]

CAESONIA [*ironically, pointing to the disorder of the room*]: Were you having a fight?

CHEREA: Yes, we were fighting.

CAESONIA [*in the same tone*]: Really? Might I know what you were fighting about?

CHEREA: About . . . nothing in particular.

CAESONIA: Ah? Then it isn't true.

CHEREA: What isn't true?

CAESONIA: You were *not* fighting.

CHEREA: Have it your own way. We weren't fighting.

CAESONIA [*smiling*]: Perhaps you'd do better to tidy up the place. Caligula hates untidiness.

HELICON [*to the Old Patrician*]: You'll end by making him do something out of character.

THE OLD PATRICIAN: Pardon . . . I don't follow. What have we done to him?

HELICON: Nothing. Just nothing. It's fantastic being futile to that point; enough to get on anybody's nerves. Try to put yourselves in Caligula's place. [*A short pause.*] I see; doing a bit of plotting, weren't you now?

THE OLD PATRICIAN: Really, that's too absurd. I hope Caligula doesn't imagine . . .

HELICON: He doesn't imagine. He *knows*. But, I suppose, at bottom, he rather wants it. . . . Well, we'd better set to tidying up.

[*All get busy.* CALIGULA *enters and watches them.*]

CALIGULA [*to the Old Patrician*]: Good day, darling. [*To the others*] Gentlemen, I'm on my way to an execution. But I thought I'd drop in at your place, Cherea, for a light meal. I've given orders to have food brought here for all of us. But send for your wives first. [*A short silence.*] Rufius should thank his stars that I've been seized with hunger. [*Confidentially*] Rufius, I may tell you, is the knight who's going to be executed. [*Another short silence.*] What's this? None of you asks me why I've sentenced him to death? [*No one speaks. Meanwhile slaves lay the table and bring food.*] Good for you! I see you're growing quite intelligent. [*He nibbles an olive.*] It has dawned on you that a man needn't have done anything for him to die. [*He stops eating and gazes at his guests with a twinkle in his eye.*] Soldiers, I am proud of you. [*Three or four women enter.*] Good! Let's take our places. Anyhow. No order of precedence today. [*All are seated.*] There's no denying it, that fellow Rufius is in luck. But I wonder if he appreciates this short reprieve. A few hours gained on death, why, they're worth their weight in gold! [*He begins eating; the others follow suit. It becomes clear that Caligula's table manners are deplorable. There is no need for him to flick his olive stones on to his neighbours' plates, or to spit out bits of gristle over the dish, or to pick his teeth with his nails, or to scratch his head furiously. However, he indulges in these practices throughout the meal, without the least compunction. At one moment he stops eating, stares at Lepidus, one of the guests, and says roughly*] You're looking grumpy, Lepidus. I wonder, can it be because I had your son killed?

LEPIDUS [*thickly*]: Certainly not, Caius. Quite the contrary.

CALIGULA [*beaming on him*]: 'Quite the contrary!' It's always nice to see a face that hides the secrets of the heart. Your face is sad. But what about your heart? Quite the contrary – isn't that so, Lepidus?

LEPIDUS [*doggedly*]: Quite the contrary, Caesar.

CALIGULA [*more and more enjoying the situation*]: Really,

Lepidus, there's no one I like better than you. Now let's have a laugh together, my dear friend. Tell me a funny story.

LEPIDUS [*who has overrated his endurance*]: Please . . .

CALIGULA: Good! Very good! Then it's I who'll tell the story. But you'll laugh, won't you, Lepidus? [*With a glint of malice*] If only for the sake of your other son. [*Smiling again*] In any case, as you've just told us, you're not in a bad humour. [*He takes a drink, then says in the tone of a teacher prompting a pupil*] Quite . . . quite the . . .

LEPIDUS [*wearily*]: Quite the contrary, Caesar.

CALIGULA: Splendid! [*Drinks again.*] Now listen. [*In a gentle, far-away tone*] Once upon a time there was a poor young emperor whom nobody loved. He loved Lepidus and, to root out of his heart his love for Lepidus, he had his youngest son killed. [*In a brisker tone*] Needless to say, there's not a word of truth in it. Still it's a funny story, eh? But you're not laughing. Nobody's laughing. Now listen! [*In a burst of anger*] I insist on everybody's laughing. You, Lepidus, shall lead the chorus. Stand up, every one of you, and laugh. [*He thumps the table.*] Do you hear what I say? I wish to see you laughing, all of you.

[*All rise to their feet. During this scene all the players, Caligula and Caesonia excepted, behave like marionettes in a puppet-play.* CALIGULA *sinks back on his couch, beaming with delight, and bursts into a fit of laughter.*]

CALIGULA: Oh, Caesonia! Just look at them! The game is up; honour, respectability, the wisdom of the nations, gone with the wind! The wind of fear has blown them all away. Fear, Caesonia – don't you agree? – is a noble emotion, pure and simple, self-sufficient, like no other; it draws its patent of nobility straight from the guts. [*He strokes his forehead and drinks again. In a friendly tone*] Well, well, let's change the subject. What have you to say, Cherea? You've been very silent.

CHEREA: I'm quite ready to speak, Caius. When you give me leave.

CALIGULA: Excellent. Then – keep silent. I'd rather have a word from our friend Mucius.

MUCIUS [*reluctantly*]: As you will, Caius.

CALIGULA: Then tell us something about your wife. And begin by sending her to this place, on my right.

[MUCIUS' WIFE *seats herself beside Caligula.*]

CALIGULA: Well, Mucius? We're waiting.

MUCIUS [*hardly knowing what he says*]: My wife . . . but . . . I'm very fond of her.

[*General laughter.*]

CALIGULA: Why, of course, my friend, of course. But how ordinary of you! So unoriginal! [*He is leaning towards her, tickling her shoulder playfully with his tongue.*] By the way, when I came in just now, you were hatching a plot, weren't you? A nice bloody little plot?

OLD PATRICIAN: Oh Caius, how can you . . . ?

CALIGULA: It doesn't matter in the least, my pet. Old age will be served. I shan't take it seriously. Not one of you has the spunk for an heroic act . . . Ah, it's just come to my mind, I have some affairs of state to settle. But, first, I've a little natural craving to relieve.

[*He rises and leads Mucius' Wife into an adjoining room.* MUCIUS *starts up from his seat.*]

CAESONIA [*amiably*]: Please, Mucius. Will you pour me out another glass of this excellent wine.

[MUCIUS *complies; his movement of revolt is quelled. Everyone looks embarrassed. Chairs creak noisily. The ensuing conversation is in a strained tone.* CAESONIA *turns to Cherea.*]

CAESONIA: Now, Cherea, suppose you tell me why you people were fighting just now?

CHEREA [*coolly*]: With pleasure, my dear Caesonia. Our

quarrel arose from a discussion whether poetry should be blood-thirsty or not.

CAESONIA: An interesting problem. Somewhat beyond my feminine comprehension, of course. Still it surprises me that your passion for art should make you come to blows.

CHEREA [*in the same rather stilted tone*]: That I can well understand. But I remember Caligula's telling me the other day that all true passion has a spice of cruelty.

CAESONIA [*helping herself from the dish in front of her*]: There's truth in that. Don't you agree, gentlemen?

THE OLD PATRICIAN: Ah, yes. Caligula has a rare insight into the secret places of the heart.

FIRST PATRICIAN: And how eloquently he spoke just now of courage!

SECOND PATRICIAN: Really he should put his ideas into writing. They would be most instructive.

CHEREA: And, what's more, it would keep him busy. It's obvious he needs something to occupy his leisure.

CAESONIA [*still eating*]: You'll be pleased to hear that Caligula shares your views; he's working on a book. Quite a big one, I believe.

[CALIGULA *enters, accompanied by* MUCIUS' WIFE.]

CALIGULA: Mucius, I return your wife, with many thanks. But excuse me, I've some orders to give. [*He hurries out.*]

[MUCIUS *has gone pale and risen to his feet.*]

CAESONIA [*to Mucius, who is standing*]: This book of his will certainly rank amongst our Latin classics. Are you listening, Mucius?

MUCIUS [*his eyes still fixed on the door by which Caligula went out*]: Yes. And what's the book about, Caesonia?

CAESONIA [*indifferently*]: Oh, it's above my head, you know.

CHEREA: May we assume it deals with the murderous power of poetry?

CAESONIA: Yes, something of that sort, I understand.

THE OLD PATRICIAN [*cheerfully*]: Well anyhow, as our friend Cherea said, it will keep him busy.

CAESONIA: Yes, my love. But I'm afraid there's one thing you won't like quite so much about this book, and that's its title.

CHEREA: What is it?

CAESONIA: 'Cold Steel.'

[CALIGULA *hurries in.*]

CALIGULA: Excuse me, but I've some urgent public work in hand. [*To the Intendant*] Intendant, you are to close the public granaries. I have signed a decree to that effect; you will find it in my study.

INTENDANT: But, sire . . .

CALIGULA: Famine begins tomorrow.

INTENDANT: But . . . but heaven knows what may happen – perhaps a revolution.

CALIGULA [*firmly and deliberately*]: I repeat; famine begins tomorrow. We all know what famine means – a national catastrophe. Well, tomorrow there will be a catastrophe, and I shall end it when I choose. After all, I haven't so many ways of proving I am free. One is always free at someone else's expense. Absurd perhaps, but so it is. [*With a keen glance at Mucius*] Apply this principle to your jealousy – and you'll understand better. [*In a meditative tone*] Still, what an ugly thing is jealousy! A disease of vanity and the imagination. One pictures one's wife . . .

[MUCIUS *clenches his fists and opens his mouth to speak. Before he can get a word out,* CALIGULA *cuts in.*]

CALIGULA: Now, gentlemen, let's go on with our meal . . . Do you know, we've been doing quite a lot of work, with Helicon's assistance? Putting the final touches to a little monograph on execution – about which you will have much to say.

HELICON: Assuming we ask your opinion.

CALIGULA: Why not be generous, Helicon, and let them into our little secrets? Come now, give them a sample. Section Three, first paragraph.

HELICON [*standing, declaims in a droning voice*]: 'Execution relieves and liberates It is universal, tonic, just in precept and in practice. A man dies because he is guilty. A man is guilty because he is one of Caligula's subjects. Now all men are Caligula's subjects. Ergo, all men are guilty and shall die. It is only a matter of time and patience.'

CALIGULA [*laughing*]: There's logic for you, don't you agree? That bit about 'patience' was rather neat, wasn't it? Allow me to tell you, that's the quality I most admire in you . . . your patience. Now, gentlemen, you can disperse. Cherea doesn't need your presence any longer. Caesonia, I wish you to stay. You too, Lepidus. Also our old friend Mereia. I want to have a little talk with you about our National Brothel. It's not functioning too well; in fact, I'm quite concerned about it.

[*The others file out slowly.* CALIGULA *follows Mucius with his eyes.*]

CHEREA: At your orders, Caius. But what's the trouble? Are the staff unsatisfactory?

CALIGULA: No, but the takings are falling off.

MEREIA: Then you should raise the entrance fee.

CALIGULA: There, Mereia, you missed a golden opportunity of keeping your mouth shut. You're too old to be interested in the subject, and I don't want your opinion.

MEREIA: Then why ask me to stay?

CALIGULA: Because, presently, I may require some cool, dispassionate advice.

[MEREIA *moves away.*]

CHEREA: If you wish to hear my views on the subject, Caius, I'd say, neither coolly nor dispassionately, that it would be a blunder to raise the scale of charges.

CALIGULA: Obviously. What's needed is a bigger turnover. I've explained my plan of campaign to Caesonia, and she will tell you all about it. Personally, I've had too much wine, I'm feeling sleepy. [*He lies down, and closes his eyes.*]

CAESONIA: It's very simple. Caligula is creating a new order of merit.

CHEREA: Sorry, I don't see the connexion.

CAESONIA: No? But there is one. It will be called the Badge of Civic Merit and awarded to those who have patronized Caligula's National Brothel most assiduously.

CHEREA: A brilliant idea!

CAESONIA: I agree. Oh, I forgot to mention that the Badge will be conferred each month, after checking the admission tickets. Any citizen who has not obtained the Badge within twelve months will be exiled, or executed.

CHEREA: Why 'or executed'?

CAESONIA: Because Caligula says it doesn't matter which – but it's important he should have the right of choosing.

CHEREA: Bravo! The Public Treasury will wipe out its deficit in no time.

[CALIGULA *has half-opened his eyes and is watching old Mereia who, standing in a corner, has produced a small flask and is sipping its contents.*]

CALIGULA [*still lying on the couch*]: What's that you're drinking, Mereia?

MEREIA: It's for my asthma, Caius.

[CALIGULA *rises and, thrusting the others aside, goes up to Mereia and sniffs his mouth.*]

CALIGULA: No, it's an antidote.

MEREIA: What an idea, Caius! You must be joking. I have choking fits at night and I've been in the doctor's hands for months.

CALIGULA: So you're afraid of being poisoned?

MEREIA: My asthma . . .

CALIGULA: No. Why beat about the bush? You're afraid I'll poison you. You suspect me. You're keeping an eye on me.

MEREIA: Good heavens, no!

CALIGULA: You suspect me. I'm not to be trusted, eh?

MEREIA: Caius!

CALIGULA [*roughly*]: Answer! [*In a cool, judicial tone*] If you take an antidote, it follows that you credit me with the intention of poisoning you. Q.E.D.

MEREIA: Yes . . . I mean . . . no!

CALIGULA: And thinking I intend to poison you, you take steps to frustrate my plan. [*He falls silent.*]

[*Meanwhile* CAESONIA *and* CHEREA *have moved away, back stage.* LEPIDUS *is watching the speakers with an air of consternation.*]

CALIGULA: That makes two crimes, Mereia, and a dilemma from which you can't escape. *Either* I have no wish to cause your death; in which case you are unjustly suspecting me, your emperor. *Or else* I desire your death; in which case, vermin that you are, you're trying to thwart my will. [*Another silence.* CALIGULA *contemplates the old man gloatingly.*] Well, Mereia, what have you to say to my logic?

MEREIA: It . . . it's sound enough, Caius. Only it doesn't apply to the case.

CALIGULA: A third crime. You take me for a fool. Now sit down and listen carefully. [*To Lepidus*] Let everyone sit down. [*To Mereia*] Of these three crimes only one does you honour; the second one – because by crediting me with a certain wish and presuming to oppose it you are deliberately defying me. You are a rebel, a leader of revolt. And that needs courage. [*Sadly*] I've a great liking for you, Mereia. And that is why you'll be condemned for crime number two, and not for either of the others. You shall die nobly, a rebel's death.

[*While he talks* MEREIA *is shrinking together on his chair.*]

CALIGULA: Don't thank me. It's quite natural. Here. [*Holds out a phial. His tone is amiable.*] Drink this poison.

[MEREIA *shakes his head. He is sobbing violently.* CALIGULA *shows signs of impatience.*]

CALIGULA: Don't waste time. Take it.

[MEREIA *makes a feeble attempt to escape. But* CALIGULA *with a wild leap is on him, catches him in the centre of the stage and after a brief struggle pins him down on a low couch. He forces the phial between his lips and smashes it with a blow of his fist. After some convulsive movements* MEREIA *dies. His face is streaming with blood and tears.* CALIGULA *rises, wipes his hands absentmindedly, then hands Mereia's flask to Caesonia.*]

CALIGULA: What was it? An antidote?

CAESONIA [*calmly*]: No, Caligula. A remedy for asthma.

[*A short silence.*]

CALIGULA [*gazing down at Mereia*]: No matter. It all comes to the same thing in the end. A little sooner, a little later . . .

[*He goes out hurriedly, still wiping his hands.*]

LEPIDUS [*in a horrified tone*]: What . . . what shall we do?

CAESONIA [*coolly*]: Remove that body to begin with, I should say. It's rather a beastly sight.

[CHEREA *and* LEPIDUS *drag the body into the wings.*]

LEPIDUS [*to Cherea*]: We must act quickly.

CHEREA: We'll need to be two hundred.

[*Young* SCIPIO *enters. Seeing Caesonia, he makes as if to leave.*]

CAESONIA: Come.

SCIPIO: What do you want?

CAESONIA: Come nearer. [*She pushes up his chin and looks him in the eyes. A short silence. Then, in a calm, unemotional voice*] He killed your father, didn't he?

SCIPIO: Yes.

CAESONIA: Do you hate him?

SCIPIO: Yes.

CAESONIA: And you'd like to kill him?

SCIPIO: Yes.

CAESONIA [*withdrawing her hand*]: But – why tell me this?

SCIPIO: Because I fear nobody. Killing him or being killed – either way out will do. And anyhow you won't betray me.

CAESONIA: That's so. I shan't betray you. But I want to tell you something – or, rather, I'd like to speak to what is best in you.

SCIPIO: What's best in me is – my hatred.

CAESONIA: Please listen carefully to what I'm going to say. It may sound hard to grasp, but it's as clear as daylight, really. And it's something that would bring about the one real revolution in this world of ours, if people would only take it in.

SCIPIO: Yes? What is it?

CAESONIA: Wait! Try to call up a picture of your father's death, of the agony on his face as they were tearing out his tongue. Think of the blood streaming from his mouth, and recall his screams, like a tortured animal's.

SCIPIO: Yes.

CAESONIA: And now think of Caligula.

SCIPIO [*his voice rough with hatred*]: Yes.

CAESONIA: Now listen. *Try to understand him.* [*She goes out, leaving* SCIPIO *gaping after her in bewilderment.*]

[HELICON *enters.*]

HELICON: Caligula will be here in a moment. Suppose you go for your meal, young poet?

SCIPIO: Helicon, help me.

HELICON: Too dangerous, my lamb. And poetry means nothing to me.

SCIPIO: You can help me. You know . . . so many things.

HELICON: I know that the days go by – and growing boys should have their meals on time . . . I know, too, that you could kill Caligula . . . and he wouldn't greatly mind it. [*Goes out.*]

[CALIGULA *enters.*]

CALIGULA: Ah, it's you, Scipio. [*He pauses. One has the impression that he is somewhat embarrassed.*] It's quite a long time since I saw you last. [*Slowly approaches Scipio.*] What have you been up to? Writing more poems, I suppose. Might I see your latest composition?

SCIPIO [*likewise ill at ease, torn between hatred and some less defined emotion*]: Yes, Caesar, I've written some more poems.

CALIGULA: On what subject?

SCIPIO: Oh, on nothing in particular. Well, on Nature in a way.

CALIGULA: A fine theme. And a vast one. And what has Nature done for you?

SCIPIO [*pulling himself together, in a somewhat truculent tone*]: It consoles me for not being Caesar.

CALIGULA: Really? And do you think Nature could console me for being Caesar?

SCIPIO [*in the same tone*]: Why not? Nature has healed worse wounds than that.

CALIGULA [*in a curiously young, unaffected voice*]: Wounds, you said? There was anger in your voice. Because I put your father to death? . . . That word you used – if you only knew how apt it is! My wounds! [*In a different tone*] Well, well, there's nothing like hatred for developing the intelligence.

SCIPIO [*stiffly*]: I answered your question about Nature.

[CALIGULA *sits down, gazes at Scipio, then brusquely grips his wrists and forces him to stand up. He takes the young man's face between his hands.*]

CALIGULA: Recite your poem to me, please.

SCIPIO: No, please, don't ask me that.

CALIGULA: Why not?

SCIPIO: I haven't got it on me.

CALIGULA: Can't you remember it?

SCIPIO: No.

CALIGULA: Anyhow you can tell me what it's about.

SCIPIO [*still hostile; reluctantly*]: I spoke of a . . . a certain harmony . . .

CALIGULA [*breaking in; in a pensive voice*]: . . . between one's feet and the earth.

SCIPIO [*looking surprised*]: Yes, it's almost that . . . and it tells of the wavy outline of the Roman hills and the sudden thrill of peace that twilight brings to them . . .

CALIGULA: And the cries of swifts thridding the green dusk.

SCIPIO [*yielding more and more to his emotion*]: Yes, yes! And that fantastic moment when the sky all flushed with red and gold swings round and shows its other side, spangled with stars.

CALIGULA: And the faint smell of smoke and trees and streams that mingles with the rising mist.

SCIPIO [*in a sort of ecstasy*]: Yes, and the chirr of crickets, the coolness veining the warm air, the rumble of carts and the farmers' shouts, dogs barking . . .

CALIGULA: And the roads drowned in shadow winding through the olive groves . . .

SCIPIO: Yes, yes. That's it, exactly. . . . But how did you know?

CALIGULA [*drawing Scipio to his breast*]: I wonder! Perhaps because the same eternal truths appeal to us both. And perhaps, too, because it's easy to share emotions – provided they are vague enough.

SCIPIO [*quivering with excitement, burying his head on Caligula's breast*]: Anyhow, what matter! All I know is that everything I feel or think of turns to love.

CALIGULA [*stroking his hair*]: That, Scipio, is a privilege of noble hearts – and how I wish I could share your . . . your limpidity! But my appetite for life's too keen; Nature can never sate it. You belong to quite another world, and you can't understand. You are single-minded for good; and I am single-minded – for evil.

SCIPIO: I *do* understand.

CALIGULA: No. There's something deep down in me – an abyss of silence, a pool of stagnant water, rotting weeds. [*With an abrupt change of manner*] Your poem sounds very good indeed, but, if you really want my opinion . . .

SCIPIO [*his head on Caligula's breast, murmurs*]: Yes?

CALIGULA: All that's a bit . . . anaemic.

SCIPIO [*recoiling abruptly, as if stung by a serpent, and gazing, horrified, at Caligula, he cries hoarsely*]: Oh, you brute! You loathsome brute! You've fooled me again. I know! You were playing a trick on me, weren't you? And now you're gloating over your success.

CALIGULA [*with a hint of sadness*]: There's truth in what you say. I *was* playing a part.

SCIPIO [*in the same indignant tone*]: What a foul, black heart you have! And how all that wickedness and hatred must make you suffer!

CALIGULA [*gently*]: That's enough.

SCIPIO: How I loathe you! And how I pity you!

CALIGULA [*angrily*]: Enough, I tell you.

SCIPIO: And how horrible a loneliness like yours must be!

CALIGULA [*in a rush of anger, gripping the boy by the collar, and shaking him*]: Loneliness! What do *you* know of it? Only the loneliness of poets and weaklings. You prate of loneliness, but you don't realize that one is *never* alone. Always we are attended by the same load of the future and the past. Those we have killed are always with us. But *they* are no great trouble. It's those we have loved, those who loved us and whom we did not love; regrets, desires, bitterness and sweetness, whores and gods, the gang celestial! Always, always with us! [*He releases Scipio and moves back to his former place.*] Alone! Ah, if only in this loneliness, this ghoul-haunted wilderness of mine, I could know, but for a moment, real solitude, real silence, the throbbing stillness of a tree! [*Sitting down, in an access of fatigue.*] Solitude? No, Scipio, mine is full of gnashings of teeth, hideous with jarring sounds and voices. And when I am with the women I make mine and darkness falls on us and I think, now my body's had its fill, that I can feel myself my own at last, poised between death and life – ah, then my solitude is fouled by the stale smell of pleasure from the woman sprawling at my side.

[*A long silence.* CALIGULA *seems weary and despondent.* SCIPIO *moves behind him and approaches hesitantly. He slowly stretches out a hand towards him, from behind, and lays it on his shoulder. Without looking round,* CALIGULA *places his hand on Scipio's.*]

SCIPIO: All men have a secret solace. It helps them to endure, and they turn to it when life has wearied them beyond enduring.

CALIGULA: Yes, Scipio.

SCIPIO: Have you nothing of the kind in your life, no refuge, no mood that makes the tears well up, no consolation?

CALIGULA: Yes, I have something of the kind.

SCIPIO: What is it?

CALIGULA [*very quietly*]: Scorn.

CURTAIN

ACT THREE

Before the curtain rises a rhythmic clash of cymbals and the thudding of a drum have been coming from the stage, and when it goes up we see a curtained-off booth, with a small proscenium in front, such as strolling players use at country fairs for an exhibition turn. On the little stage are CAESONIA *and* HELICON, *flanked by cymbal-players. Seated on benches, with their backs to the audience, are some* PATRICIANS *and young* SCIPIO.

HELICON [*in the tone of a showman at a fair*]: Walk up! Walk up! [*A clash of cymbals.*] Once more the gods have come to earth. They have assumed the human form of our heaven-born emperor, known to men as Caligula. Draw near, mortals of common clay; a holy miracle is taking place before your eyes. By a divine dispensation peculiar to Caligula's hallowed reign, the secrets of the gods will be revealed to you. [*Cymbals.*]

CAESONIA: Come, gentlemen. Come and adore him – and don't forget to give your alms. Today heaven and its mysteries are on show, at a price to suit every pocket.

HELICON: For all to see, the secrets of Olympus, revelations in high places, featuring gods in undress, their little plots and pranks. Step this way! The whole truth about your gods! [*Cymbals.*]

CAESONIA: Adore him, and give your alms. Come near, gentlemen. The show's beginning.

[*Cymbals.* SLAVES *are placing various objects on the platform.*]

HELICON: An epoch-making reproduction of the life celestial, warranted authentic in every detail. For the first time the pomp and splendour of the gods are presented to the Roman public. You will relish our novel, breathtaking effects: flashes of lightning [SLAVES *light Greek fires*], peals of thunder [*they roll a barrel filled with stones*], the divine event on its triumphal way. Now watch with all your eyes. [*He draws aside the curtain.*]

[*Grotesquely attired as Venus,* CALIGULA *beams down on them from a pedestal.*]

CALIGULA: I'm Venus today.

CAESONIA: Now for the adoration. Bow down. [*All but* SCIPIO *bend their heads.*] And repeat after me the litany of Venus yclept Caligula.

'Our Lady of pangs and pleasures . . .'

THE PATRICIANS: 'Our Lady of pangs and pleasures . . .'

CAESONIA: 'Born of the waves, bitter and bright with seafoam . . .'

THE PATRICIANS: 'Born of the waves, bitter and bright with seafoam . . .'

CAESONIA: 'O Queen whose gifts are laughter and regrets . . .'

THE PATRICIANS: 'O Queen whose gifts are laughter and regrets . . .'

CAESONIA: 'Rancours and raptures . . .'

THE PATRICIANS: 'Rancours and raptures . . .'

CAESONIA: 'Teach us the indifference that kindles love anew . . .'

THE PATRICIANS: 'Teach us the indifference that kindles love anew . . .'

CAESONIA: 'Make known to us the truth about this world – which is that it has none . . .'

THE PATRICIANS: 'Make known to us the truth about this world – which is that it has none . . .'

CAESONIA: 'And grant us strength to live up to this verity of verities.'

THE PATRICIANS: 'And grant us strength to live up to this verity of verities.'

CAESONIA: Now, pause.

THE PATRICIANS: Now pause.

CAESONIA [*after a short silence*]: 'Bestow your gifts on us, and shed on our faces the light of your impartial cruelty, your wanton hatred; unfold above our eyes your arms laden with flowers and murders . . .'

THE PATRICIANS: '. . . your arms laden with flowers and murders.'

CAESONIA: 'Welcome your wandering children home, to the bleak sanctuary of your heartless, thankless love. Give us your passions without object, your griefs devoid of reason, your raptures that lead nowhere . . .'

THE PATRICIANS: '. . . your raptures that lead nowhere . . .'

CAESONIA [*raising her voice*]: 'O Queen, so empty yet so ardent, inhuman yet so earthly, make us drunk with the wine of your equivalence, and surfeit us for ever in the brackish darkness of your heart.'

THE PATRICIANS: 'Make us drunk with the wine of your equivalence, and surfeit us for ever in the brackish darkness of your heart.'

[*When the* PATRICIANS *have said the last response,* CALIGULA, *who until now has been quite motionless, snorts and rises.*]

CALIGULA [*in a stentorian voice*]: Granted, my children. Your prayer is heard. [*He squats cross-legged on the pedestal.*]

[*One by one the* PATRICIANS *make obeisance, deposit their alms, and line up on the right. The last, in his flurry, forgets to make an offering.* CALIGULA *bounds to his feet.*]

CALIGULA: Steady! Steady on! Come here, my lad. Worship's very well, but almsgiving is better. Thank you, We are appeased. Ah, if the gods had no wealth other than the love you mortals give them, they'd be as poor as poor Caligula. Now, gentlemen, you may go, and spread abroad the glad tidings of the miracle you've been allowed to witness. You have seen Venus, seen her godhead with your fleshly eyes, and Venus herself has spoken to you. Go, most favoured gentlemen.

[*The* PATRICIANS *begin to move away.*]

CALIGULA: Just a moment. When you leave, mind you take the exit on your left. I have posted sentries in the others, with orders to kill you.

[*The* PATRICIANS *file out hastily in some disorder. The* SLAVES *and* MUSICIANS *leave the stage.*]

HELICON [*pointing a monitory finger at Scipio*]: Naughty boy, you've been playing the anarchist again.

SCIPIO [*to Caligula*]: You spoke blasphemy, Caius.

CALIGULA: Blasphemy? What's that?

SCIPIO: You're befouling heaven, after bloodying the earth.

CALIGULA: How this youngster loves big words! [*He stretches himself on a couch.*]

CAESONIA [*composedly*]: You should watch your tongue, my lad. At this moment men are dying in Rome for saying much less.

SCIPIO: Maybe – but I've resolved to tell Caligula the truth.

CAESONIA: Hark at him, Caligula! That was the one thing missing in your Empire – a bold young moralist.

CALIGULA [*giving Scipio a curious glance*]: Do you really believe in the gods, Scipio?

SCIPIO: No.

CALIGULA: Then I fail to follow. If you don't believe, why be so keen to scent out blasphemy?

SCIPIO: One may deny something without feeling called on to besmirch it, or deprive others of the right of believing in it.

CALIGULA: But that's humility, the real thing, unless I'm much mistaken. Ah, my dear Scipio, how glad I am on your behalf – and a trifle envious, too. Humility's the one emotion I may never feel.

SCIPIO: It's not I you're envious of; it's the gods.

CALIGULA: If you don't mind, that will remain our secret – the great enigma of our reign. Really, you know, there's only one thing for which I might be blamed today – and that's this small advance I've made upon the path of freedom. For someone who loves power the rivalry of the gods is rather irksome. Well, I've proved to these imaginary gods that any man, without previous training, if he applies his mind to it, can play their absurd parts to perfection.

SCIPIO: That, Caius, is what I meant by blasphemy.

CALIGULA: No, Scipio, it's clear-sightedness. I've merely realized that there's only one way of getting even with the gods. All that's needed is to be as cruel as they.

SCIPIO: All that's needed is to play the tyrant.

CALIGULA: Tell me, my young friend. What exactly *is* a tyrant?

SCIPIO: A blind soul.

CALIGULA: That's a moot point. I should say the real tyrant is a man who sacrifices a whole nation to his ideal or his ambition. But I have no ideal, and there's nothing left for me to covet by way of power or glory. If I use this power of mine, it's to compensate.

SCIPIO: For what?

CALIGULA: For the hatred and stupidity of the gods.

SCIPIO: Hatred does not compensate for hatred. Power is no solution. Personally I know only one way of countering the hostility of the world we live in.

CALIGULA: Yes? And what is it?

SCIPIO: Poverty.

CALIGULA [*bending over his feet and scrutinizing his toes*]: I must try that, too.

SCIPIO: Meanwhile many men round you are dying.

CALIGULA: Oh, come! Not so many as all that. Do you know how many wars I've refused to embark on?

SCIPIO: No.

CALIGULA: Three. And do you know why I refused?

SCIPIO: Because the grandeur of Rome means nothing to you.

CALIGULA: No. Because I respect human life.

SCIPIO: You're joking, Caius.

CALIGUA: Or, anyhow, I respect it more than I respect military triumphs. But it's a fact that I don't respect it more than I respect my own life. And if I find killing easy, it's because dying isn't hard for me. No, the more I think about it, the surer I feel that I'm no tyrant.

SCIPIO: What matter, if it costs us quite as dear as if you were one?

CALIGULA [*with a hint of petulance*]: If you had the least head for figures you'd know that the smallest war a tyrant – however level-headed he might be – indulged in would cost you a thousand times more than all my vagaries (shall we call them?) put together.

SCIPIO: Possibly. But at least there'd be *some* sense behind a war; it would be understandable – and to understand makes up for much.

CALIGULA: There's no understanding Fate; therefore I choose to play the part of Fate. I wear the foolish, unintelligible face of a professional god. And that is what the men who were here with you have learnt to adore.

SCIPIO: That, too, Caius, is blasphemy.

CALIGULA: No, Scipio, it's dramatic art. The great mistake you people make is not to take the drama seriously enough. If you did, you'd know that any man can play lead in the divine comedy and become a god. All he needs do is to harden his heart.

SCIPIO: You may be right, Caius. But I rather think you've done everything that was needed to rouse up against you a legion of human gods, ruthless as yourself, who will drown in blood your godhead of a day.

CAESONIA: Really, Scipio!

CALIGULA [*peremptorily*]: No, don't stop him, Caesonia. Yes, Scipio, you spoke truer than you knew; I've done everything needed to that end. I find it hard to picture the event you speak of – but I sometimes dream it. And in all those faces surging up out of the angry darkness, convulsed with fear and hatred, I see, and I rejoice to see, the only god I've worshipped on this earth; foul and craven as the human heart. [*Irritably*] Now go. I've had enough of you, more than enough. [*In a different tone*] I really must attend to my toe-nails; they're not nearly red enough, and I've no time to waste.

[*All go, with the exception of* HELICON. *He hovers round Caligula, who is busy painting his toe-nails.*]

CALIGULA: Helicon!

HELICON: Yes?

CALIGULA: Getting on with your task?

HELICON: What task?

CALIGULA: You know . . . the moon.

HELICON: Ah yes, the moon. . . . It's a matter of time and patience. But I'd like to have a word with you.

CALIGULA: I might have patience; only I have not much time. So you must make haste.

HELICON: I said I'd do my utmost. But, first, I have something to tell you. Very serious news.

CALIGULA [*as if he has not heard*]: Mind you, I've had her already.

HELICON: Whom?

CALIGULA: The moon.

HELICON: Yes, yes ... Now listen please. Do you know there's a plot being hatched against your life?

CALIGULA: What's more, I had her thoroughly. Only two or three times, to be sure. Still, I had her all right.

HELICON: For the last hour I've been trying to tell you about it, only –

CALIGULA: It was last summer. I'd been gazing at her so long, and stroking her so often on the marble pillars in the gardens that evidently she'd come to understand.

HELICON: Please stop trifling, Caius. Even if you refuse to listen, it's my duty to tell you this. And if you shut your ears, it can't be helped.

CALIGULA [*varnishing his toe-nails*]: This varnish is no good at all. But, to come back to the moon – it was a cloudless August night.

[HELICON *looks sulkily away, and keeps silence.*]

CALIGULA: She was coy, to begin with. I'd gone to bed. First she was blood-red, low on the horizon. Then she began rising, quicker and quicker, growing brighter and brighter all the while. And the higher she climbed, the paler she grew, till she was like a milky pool in a dark wood rustling with stars. Slowly, shyly she approached, through the warm night-air, soft, light as gossamer, naked in beauty. She crossed the threshold of my room, glided to my bed, poured herself into it, and flooded me with her smiles and sheen. . . . No, really this new varnish is a failure. . . . So you see, Helicon, I can say, without boasting, that I've had her.

HELICON: Now will you listen, and learn the danger that's threatening you?

CALIGULA [*ceasing to fiddle with his toes, and gazing at him fixedly*]: All I want, Helicon, is – the moon. For the rest, I've always known what will kill me. I haven't yet exhausted all that is to keep me living. That's why I want the moon. And you must not return till you have secured her for me.

HELICON: Very well. . . . Now I'll do my duty and tell you what I've learnt. There's a plot against you. Cherea is the ringleader. I came across this tablet which tells you all you need to know. See, I put it here. [*He places the tablet on one of the seats and moves away.*]

CALIGULA: Where are you off to, Helicon?

HELICON [*from the threshold*]: To get the moon for you.

[*There is a mouse-like scratching at the opposite door.* CALIGULA *swings round and sees the Old Patrician.*]

THE OLD PATRICIAN [*timidly*]: May I, Caius . . .

CALIGULA [*impatiently*]: Come in! Come in! [*Gazes at him.*] So, my pet, you've returned to have another look at Venus.

THE OLD PATRICIAN: Well . . . no. It's not quite that. Ssh! Oh, sorry, Caius! I only wanted to say . . . You know I'm very, very devoted to you – and my one desire is to end my days in peace.

CALIGULA: Be quick, man. Get it out!

THE OLD PATRICIAN: Well, it's . . . it's like this. [*Hurriedly*] It's terribly serious, that's what I meant to say.

CALIGULA: No, it isn't serious.

THE OLD PATRICIAN: But – I don't follow. *What* isn't serious?

CALIGULA: But what are we talking about, my love?

THE OLD PATRICIAN [*glancing nervously round the room*]: I mean to say . . . [*Wriggles, shuffles, then bursts out with it*] There's a plot afoot, against you.

CALIGULA: There! You see. Just as I said; it isn't serious.

THE OLD PATRICIAN: But, Caius, they mean to kill you.

CALIGULA [*approaching him and grasping his shoulders*]: Do you know why I can't believe you?

THE OLD PATRICIAN [*raising an arm, as if to take an oath*]: The gods bear witness, Caius, that . . .

CALIGULA [*gently but firmly pressing him back towards the door*]: Don't swear. I particularly ask you not to swear. Listen, instead. Suppose it were true, what you are telling me – I'd have to assume you were betraying your friends, isn't that so?

THE OLD PATRICIAN [*flustered*]: Well, Caius, considering the deep affection I have for you . . .

CALIGULA [*in the same tone as before*]: And I cannot assume *that.* I've always loathed baseness of that sort so profoundly that I could never restrain myself from having a betrayer put to death. But I know the man you are, my worthy friend. And I'm convinced you neither wish to play the traitor nor to die.

THE OLD PATRICIAN: Certainly not, Caius. Most certainly not.

CALIGULA: So you see I was right in refusing to believe you. You wouldn't stoop to baseness, would you?

THE OLD PATRICIAN: Oh no, indeed!

CALIGULA: Nor betray your friends?

THE OLD PATRICIAN: I need hardly tell you that, Caius.

CALIGULA: Therefore it follows that there isn't any plot. It was just a joke – between ourselves, rather a silly joke – what you've just been telling me, eh?

THE OLD PATRICIAN [*feebly*]: Yes, yes. A joke, merely a joke.

CALIGULA: Good. So now we know where we are. Nobody wants to kill me.

THE OLD PATRICIAN: Nobody. That's it. Nobody at all.

CALIGULA [*drawing a deep breath; in measured tones*]: Then – leave me, sweetheart. A man of honour is an animal so rare in the present-day world that I couldn't bear the sight of one too long. I must be left alone to relish this unique experience.

[*The Old Patrician goes out. For some moments* CALIGULA *gazes, without moving, at the tablet. He picks it up and reads it. Then, again, draws a deep breath. Then summons a palace guard.*]

CALIGULA: Bring Cherea to me.

[*The man starts to leave.*]

CALIGULA: Wait!

[*The man halts.*]

CALIGULA: Treat him politely.

[*The man goes out.* CALIGULA *falls to pacing the room. After a while he approaches the mirror.*]

CALIGULA: You decided to be logical, didn't you, poor simpleton? Logic for ever! The question now is: Where will that take you? [*Ironically*] Suppose the moon were brought here, everything would be different. That was the idea, wasn't it? Then the impossible would become possible, in a flash the Great Change come, and all things be transfigured. After all, why shouldn't Helicon bring it off? One night, perhaps, he'll catch her sleeping in a lake, and carry her here, trapped in a glistening net, all slimy with weeds and water, like a pale bloated fish drawn from the depths. Why not, Caligula? Why not, indeed? [*He casts a glance round the room.*] Fewer and fewer people round me; I wonder why. [*Addressing the mirror, in a muffled voice*] Too many dead, too many dead – that makes an emptiness. . . . No, even if the moon were mine, I could not retrace my way. Even were those dead men thrilling again under the sun's caress, the murders wouldn't go back underground for that. [*Angrily*] Logic, Caligula; follow where logic leads. Power to the uttermost; wilfulness without end. Ah, I'm the only man on earth to know the secret – that power can never be complete without a total self-surrender to the dark impulse of one's destiny. No there's no return. I must go on and on, until the consummation.

[CHEREA *enters.* CALIGULA *is slumped in his chair, the cloak drawn tightly round him.*]

CHEREA: You sent for me, Caius?

CALIGULA [*languidly*]: Yes, Cherea.

[*A short silence.*]

CHEREA: Have you anything particular to tell me?

CALIGULA: No, Cherea.

[*Another silence.*]

CHEREA [*with a hint of petulance*]: Are you sure you really need my presence?

CALIGULA: Absolutely sure, Cherea. [*Another silence. Then, as if suddenly recollecting himself.*] I'm sorry for seeming so inhospitable. I was following up my thoughts, and – Now do sit down, we'll have a friendly little chat. I'm in a mood for some intelligent conversation.

[CHEREA *sits down. For the first time since the play began,* CALIGULA *gives the impression of being his natural self.*]

CALIGULA: Do you think, Cherea, that it's possible for two men of much the same temperament and equal pride to talk to each other with complete frankness – if only once in their lives? Can they strip themselves naked, so to speak, and shed their prejudices, their private interests, the lies by which they live?

CHEREA: Yes, Caius, I think it possible. But I don't think you'd be capable of it.

CALIGULA: You're right. I only wished to know if you agreed with me. So let's wear our masks, and muster up our lies. And we'll talk as fencers fight, padded on all the vital parts. Tell me, Cherea, why don't you like me?

CHEREA: Because there's nothing likeable about you, Caius. Because such feelings can't be had to order. And because

I understand you far too well. One cannot like an aspect of oneself which one always tries to keep concealed.

CALIGULA: But why is it you hate me?

CHEREA: There, Caius, you're mistaken. I do not hate you. I regard you as noxious and cruel, vain and selfish. But I cannot hate you, because I don't think you are happy. And I cannot scorn you, because I know you are no coward.

CALIGULA: Then why wish to kill me?

CHEREA: I've told you why; because I regard you as noxious, a constant menace. I like, and need, to feel secure. So do most men. They resent living in a world where the most preposterous fancy may at any moment become a reality, and the absurd transfix their lives, like a dagger in the heart. I feel as they do; I refuse to live in a topsy-turvy world. I want to know where I stand, and to stand secure.

CALIGULA Security and logic don't go together.

CHEREA: Quite true. My plan of life may not be logical, but at least it's sound.

CALIGULA: Go on.

CHEREA: There's no more to say. I'll be no party to your logic. I've a very different notion of my duties as a man. And I know that the majority of your subjects share my view. You outrage their deepest feelings. It's only natural that you should . . . disappear.

CALIGULA: I see your point, and it's legitimate enough. For most men, I grant you, it's obvious. But *you*, I should have thought, would have known better. You're an intelligent man, and given intelligence, one has a choice: either to pay its price or to disown it. Why do you shirk the issue and neither disown it nor consent to pay its price?

CHEREA: Because what I want is to live, and to be happy. Neither, to my mind, is possible if one pushes the absurd to its logical conclusions. As you see, I'm quite an ordinary sort of man. True, there are moments when, to feel free of them, I desire the death of those I love, or I hanker after women from whom the ties of family or friendship debar me. Were logic everything, I'd kill or fornicate on such occasions. But I consider that these passing fancies have no great importance. If everyone set to gratifying them, the world would be impossible to live in, and happiness, too, would go by the board. And these, I repeat, are the things that count, for me.

CALIGULA: So, I take it, you believe in some higher principle?

CHEREA: Certainly I believe that some actions are – shall I say? – more praiseworthy than others.

CALIGULA: And *I* believe that all are on an equal footing.

CHEREA: I know it, Caius, and that's why I don't hate you. I understand and, to a point, agree with you. But you're pernicious, and you've got to go.

CALIGULA: True enough. But why risk your life by telling me this?

CHEREA: Because others will take my place, and because I don't like lying.

[*A short silence.*]

CALIGULA: Cherea!

CHEREA: Yes, Caius?

CALIGULA: Do you think that two men of similar temperament and equal pride can, if only once in their lives, open their hearts to each other?

CHEREA: That, I believe, is what we've just been doing.

CALIGULA: Yes, Cherea. But you thought I was incapable of it.

CHEREA: I was wrong, Caius. I admit it, and I thank you. Now I await your sentence.

CALIGULA: My sentence? Ah, I see. [*Producing the tablet from under his cloak*] You know what this is, Cherea?

CHEREA: I knew you had it.

CALIGULA [*passionately*]: You knew I had it! So your frankness was all a piece of play-acting. The two friends did *not* open their hearts to each other. Well, well! It's no great matter. Now we can stop playing at sincerity, and resume life on the old footing. But first I'll ask you to make just one more effort; to bear with my caprices and my tactlessness a little longer. Listen well, Cherea. This tablet is the one and only piece of evidence against you.

CHEREA: Caius, I'd rather go. I'm sick and tired of all these antics. Only too well I know them, and I've had enough. Let me go, please.

CALIGULA [*in the same tense, passionate voice*]: No, stay. This tablet is the only evidence. Is that clear?

CHEREA: Evidence? I never knew you needed evidence to send a man to his death.

CALIGULA: That's true. Still, for once I wish to contradict myself. Nobody can object to that. It's so pleasant to contradict oneself occasionally; so restful. And I need rest, Cherea.

CHEREA: I don't follow . . . and, frankly, I've no taste for these subtleties.

CALIGULA: I know, Cherea, I know. You're not like me; you're an ordinary man, sound in mind and body. And naturally you've no desire for the extraordinary. [*With a burst of laughter*] You want to live and to be happy. That's all!

CHEREA: I think, Caius, we'd better leave it at that. . . . Can I go?

CALIGULA: Not yet. A little patience, if you don't mind – I shall not keep you long. You see this thing – this piece of evidence? I choose to assume that I can't sentence you to death without it. That's my idea . . . and my repose. Well! See what becomes of evidence in an emperor's hands. [*He holds the tablet to a torch.*]

[CHEREA *approaches. The torch is between them. The tablet begins to melt.*]

CALIGULA: You see, conspirator! The tablet's melting, and as it melts a look of innocence is dawning on your face. What a handsome forehead you have, Cherea! And how rare, how beautiful a sight is an innocent man! Admire my power. Even the gods cannot restore innocence without first punishing the culprit. But your emperor needs only a torch-flame to absolve you and give you a new lease of hope. So carry on, Cherea; follow out the noble precepts we've been hearing, wherever they may take you. Meanwhile your emperor awaits his repose. It's his way of living and being happy.

[CHEREA *stares, dumbfounded, at Caligula. He makes a vague gesture, seems to understand, opens his mouth to speak – and walks abruptly away. Smiling, holding the tablet to the flame,* CALIGULA *follows the receding figure with his gaze.*]

CURTAIN

ACT FOUR

The stage is in semi-darkness. CHEREA *and* SCIPIO *enter.* CHEREA *crosses right, then comes back left to Scipio.*

SCIPIO [*sulkily*]: What do you want of me?

CHEREA: There's no time to lose. And we must know our minds, we must be resolute.

SCIPIO: Who says I'm not resolute?

CHEREA: You didn't attend our meeting yesterday.

SCIPIO [*looking away*]: That's so, Cherea.

CHEREA: Scipio, I am older than you, and I'm not in the habit of asking others' help. But, I won't deny it, I need you now. This murder needs honourable men to sponsor it. Amongst all these wounded vanities and sordid fears, our motives only, yours and mine, are disinterested. Of course I know that, if you leave us, we can count on your silence. But that is not the point. What I want is – for you to stay with us.

SCIPIO: I understand. But I can't, oh no, I *cannot* do as you wish.

CHEREA: So you are with him?

SCIPIO: No. But I cannot be against him. [*Pauses; then in a muffled voice*] Even if I killed him, my heart would still be with him.

CHEREA: And yet – he killed your father!

SCIPIO: Yes – and that's how it all began. But that, too, is how it ends.

CHEREA: He denies what you believe in. He tramples on all that you hold sacred.

SCIPIO: I know, Cherea. And yet something inside me

is akin to him. The same fire burns in both our hearts.

CHEREA: There are times when a man must make his choice. Personally I have silenced in my heart all that might be akin to him.

SCIPIO: But – *I* – I cannot make a choice. I have my own sorrow, but I suffer with him, too; I share his pain. I understand all – that is my trouble.

CHEREA: So that's it. You have chosen to take his side.

SCIPIO [*passionately*]: No, Cherea. I beg you, don't think that. I can never, never again take anybody's side.

CHEREA [*affectionately; approaching Scipio*]: Do you know, I hate him even more for having made of you – what he has made.

SCIPIO: Yes, he has taught me to expect everything of life.

CHEREA: No, he has taught you despair. And to have instilled despair into a young heart is fouler than the foulest of the crimes he has committed up to now. I assure you, *that* alone would justify me in killing him out of hand. [*He goes towards the door.*]

[HELICON *enters.*]

HELICON: I've been hunting for you high and low, Cherea. Caligula's giving a little party here, for his personal friends only. Naturally he expects you to attend it. [*To Scipio*] You, my boy, aren't wanted. Off you go!

SCIPIO [*looking back at Cherea, as he goes out*]: Cherea.

CHEREA [*gently*]: Yes, Scipio?

SCIPIO: Try to understand.

CHEREA [*in the same gentle tone*]: No, Scipio.

[SCIPIO *and* HELICON *go out. A clash of arms in the wings. Two soldiers enter right, escorting the* OLD PATRICIAN *and the* FIRST PATRICIAN, *who show signs of alarm.*]

FIRST PATRICIAN [*to one of the soldiers, in a tone which he vainly tries to steady*]: But . . . but what *can* he want with us at this hour of the night?

SOLDIER: Sit there. [*Points to the chairs on the right.*]

FIRST PATRICIAN: If it's only to have us killed – like so many others – why all these preliminaries?

SOLDIER: Sit down, you old mule.

THE OLD PATRICIAN: Better do as he says. It's clear he doesn't know anything.

SOLDIER: Yes, darling, quite clear. [*Goes out.*]

FIRST PATRICIAN: We should have acted sooner; I always said so. Now we're for the torture chamber.

[*The* SOLDIER *comes back with* CHEREA, *then goes out.*]

CHEREA [*seating himself. He shows no sign of apprehension*]: Any idea what's happening?

FIRST PATRICIAN AND THE OLD PATRICIAN [*speaking together*]: He's found out about the conspiracy.

CHEREA: Yes? And then?

THE OLD PATRICIAN [*shuddering*]: The torture chamber for us all.

CHEREA [*still unperturbed*]: I remember that Caligula once gave 81,000 sesterces to a slave who, though he was tortured nearly to death, wouldn't confess to a theft he had committed.

FIRST PATRICIAN: A lot of consolation that is – for us!

CHEREA: Anyhow it shows that he appreciates courage. What's more, when he was asked, 'Why 81,000 sesterces?' he answered, 'And why 80,000 or 79,000?' [*To the Old Patrician*] Would you very much mind not chattering with your teeth? It's a noise I particularly dislike.

THE OLD PATRICIAN: I'm sorry, but –

FIRST PATRICIAN: Enough trifling! Our lives are at stake.

CHEREA [*coolly*]: Do you know Caligula's favourite remark?

THE OLD PATRICIAN [*on the verge of tears*]: Yes. He says to the executioner, 'Kill him slowly, so that he feels what dying's like!'

CHEREA: No, there's a better one. After an execution he yawns, and says quite seriously: 'What I admire most is my imperturbability.'

FIRST PATRICIAN: Do you hear . . . ?

[*A clanking of weapons is heard off-stage.*]

CHEREA: That remark betrays a weakness in his make-up.

THE OLD PATRICIAN: Would you be kind enough to stop philosophizing? It's something I particularly dislike.

[*A* SLAVE *enters and deposits a sheaf of knives on a seat.*]

CHEREA [*who has not noticed him*]: Philosophizing? I should hardly call it that. Still, there's no denying it's remarkable, the effect this man has on all with whom he comes in contact. He forces one to think. There's nothing like insecurity for stimulating the brain. That, of course, is why he's so much hated.

THE OLD PATRICIAN [*pointing a trembling finger*]: Look!

CHEREA [*noticing the knives, in a slightly altered tone*]: Perhaps you were right.

FIRST PATRICIAN: Yes, waiting was a mistake. We should have acted at once.

CHEREA: I agree. Wisdom's come too late.

THE OLD PATRICIAN: But it's . . . it's crazy. I don't want to die. [*He rises and begins to edge away. Two* SOLDIERS *appear and, after slapping his face, force him back on to his seat.*]

[*The* FIRST PATRICIAN *squirms in his chair.* CHEREA *utters some inaudible words. Suddenly a queer music begins behind the curtain at the back of the stage: a thrumming and tinkling of zithers and cymbals. The* PATRICIANS *gaze at each other in silence. Outlined on the illuminated curtain, in shadow-play,* CALIGULA *appears, makes some grotesque dance movements, and retreats from view. He is wearing ballet-dancer's skirts and his head is garlanded with flowers. A moment later a* SOLDIER *announces gravely*, 'Gentlemen, the performance is over.' *Meanwhile* CAESONIA *has entered soundlessly behind the watching Patricians. She speaks in an ordinary voice, but none the less they give a start on hearing it.*]

CAESONIA: Caligula has instructed me to tell you that, whereas in the past he always summoned you for affairs of state, today he invited you to share with him an artistic emotion. [*A short pause. Then she continues in the same tone*] He added, I may say, that anyone who has not shared in it will be beheaded. [*They keep silent.*] I apologize for insisting; but I must ask you if you found that dance beautiful.

FIRST PATRICIAN [*after a brief hesitation*]: Yes, Caesonia. It was beautiful.

THE OLD PATRICIAN [*effusively*]: Lovely! Lovely!

CAESONIA: And you, Cherea?

CHEREA [*icily*]: It was . . . very high art.

CAESONIA: Good. Now I can describe your artistic emotions to Caligula. [*Goes out.*]

CHEREA: And now we must act quickly. You two stay here. Before the night is out there'll be a hundred of us. [*He goes out.*]

THE OLD PATRICIAN: No, no. *You* stay. Let me go, instead. [*Sniffs the air.*] It smells of death here.

FIRST PATRICIAN: And of lies. [*Sadly*] I said that dance was beautiful!

THE OLD PATRICIAN [*conciliatingly*]: And so it was, in a way. Most original.

[*Some* PATRICIANS *and* KNIGHTS *enter hurriedly.*]

SECOND PATRICIAN: What's on foot? Do you know anything? The Emperor's summoned us here.

THE OLD PATRICIAN [*absentmindedly*]: For a dance, maybe.

SECOND PATRICIAN: What dance?

THE OLD PATRICIAN: Well, I mean . . . er . . . the artistic emotion.

THIRD PATRICIAN: I've been told Caligula's very ill.

FIRST PATRICIAN: He's a sick man, yes . . .

THIRD PATRICIAN: What's he suffering from? [*In a joyful tone*] By God, is he going to die?

FIRST PATRICIAN: I doubt it. His disease is fatal – to others only.

THE OLD PATRICIAN: That's one way of putting it.

SECOND PATRICIAN: Quite so. But hasn't he some other disease less serious, and more to our advantage?

FIRST PATRICIAN: No. That malady of his excludes all others. [*He goes out.*]

[CAESONIA *enters. A short silence.*]

CAESONIA [*in a casual tone*]: If you want to know, Caligula has stomach trouble. Just now he vomited blood.

[*The* PATRICIANS *crowd round her.*]

SECOND PATRICIAN: O mighty gods, I vow, if he recovers, to pay the Treasury two hundred thousand sesterces as a token of my joy.

THIRD PATRICIAN [*with exaggerated eagerness*]: O Jupiter, take my life in place of his!

[CALIGULA *has entered, and is listening.*]

CALIGULA [*going up to the Second Patrician*]: I accept your offer, Lucius. And I thank you. My Treasurer will call on you tomorrow. [*Goes to the Third Patrician and embraces him.*] You can't imagine how touched I am. [*A short silence. Then, tenderly*] So you love me, Cassius, as much as that?

THIRD PATRICIAN [*emotionally*]: Oh Caesar, there's nothing, nothing I wouldn't sacrifice for your sake.

CALIGULA [*embracing him again*]: Ah Cassius, this is really too much; I don't deserve all this love.

[CASSIUS *makes a protesting gesture.*]

CALIGULA: No, no, really I don't! I'm not worthy of it.

[*He beckons to two soldiers.*] Take him away. [*Gently, to Cassius*] Go, dear friend, and remember that Caligula has lost his heart to you.

THIRD PATRICIAN [*vaguely uneasy*]: But – where are they taking me?

CALIGULA: Why, to your death, of course. Your generous offer was accepted, and I feel better already. Even that nasty taste of blood in my mouth has gone. You've cured me, Cassius. It's been miraculous, and how proud you must feel of having worked the miracle of laying your life down for your friend – especially when that friend's none other than Caligula! So now you see me quite myself again, and ready for a festive night.

THIRD PATRICIAN [*shrieking, as he is dragged away*]: No! No! I don't want to die. You can't be serious!

CALIGULA [*in a thoughtful voice, between the shrieks*]: Soon the sea-roads will be golden with mimosas. The women will wear their lightest dresses. And the sky! Ah Cassius, what a blaze of clean, swift sunshine! The smiles of life. [*Cassius is near the door.* CALIGULA *gives him a gentle push. Suddenly his tone grows serious.*] Life, my friend, is something to be cherished. Had you cherished it enough, you wouldn't have gambled it away so rashly. [*Cassius is led off.* CALIGULA *returns to the table.*] The loser must pay. There's no alternative. [*A short silence.*] Come, Caesonia. [*He turns to the others.*] By the bye, an idea has just waylaid me, and it's such an apt one that I want to share it with you. Until now my reign has been too happy. There's been no world-wide plague, no religious persecution, not even a rebellion – nothing in fact to make us memorable. And that, I'd have you know, is why I try to remedy the stinginess of Fate. I mean – I don't know if you've followed me – that, well [*he gives a little laugh*], it's I who replace the epidemics that we've missed. [*In a different tone*] That's enough. I see Cherea's coming. Your turn, Caesonia. [*Goes out.*]

[CHEREA *and the* FIRST PATRICIAN *enter.* CAESONIA *hurries towards Cherea.*]

CAESONIA: Caligula is dead. [*She turns her head, as if to hide her tears; her eyes are fixed on the others, who keep silence. Everyone looks horrified, but for different reasons.*]

FIRST PATRICIAN: You . . . you're *sure* this dreadful thing has happened? It seems incredible. Only a short while ago he was dancing.

CAESONIA: Quite so – and the effort was too much for him.

[CHEREA *moves hastily from one man to the other. No one speaks.*]

CAESONIA: You've nothing to say, Cherea?

CHEREA [*in a low voice*]: It's a great misfortune for us all, Caesonia.

[CALIGULA *bursts in violently and goes up to Cherea.*]

CALIGULA: Well played, Cherea. [*He spins round and stares at the others. Petulantly*] Too bad! It didn't come off. [*To Caesonia*] Don't forget what I told you. [*Goes out.*]

[CAESONIA *stares after him without speaking.*]

THE OLD PATRICIAN [*hoping against hope*]: Is he ill, Caesonia?

CAESONIA [*with a hostile look*]: No, my pet. But what you don't know is that the man never has more than two hours' sleep and spends the best part of the night roaming about the corridors in his Palace. Another thing you don't know – and you've never given a thought to – is what may pass in this man's mind in those deadly hours between midnight and sunrise. Is he ill? No, not ill – unless you invent a name and medicine for the black ulcers that fester in his soul.

CHEREA [*seemingly affected by her words*]: You're right, Caesonia. We all know that Caius . . .

CAESONIA [*breaking in, emotionally*]: Yes, you know it – in your fashion. But, like all those who have none, you can't abide anyone who has too much soul. Healthy people loathe invalids. Happy people hate the sad. Too much soul! That's what bites you, isn't it? You prefer to label it a disease; that way all the dolts are justified and pleased. [*In a changed tone*] Tell me, Cherea. Has love ever meant anything to you?

CHEREA [*himself again*]: I'm afraid we're too old now, Caesonia, to learn the art of love-making. And anyhow it's highly doubtful if Caligula will give us time to do so.

CAESONIA [*who has recovered her composure*]: True enough. [*She sits down.*] Oh, I was forgetting . . . Caligula asked me to impart some news to you. You know, perhaps, that it's a red-letter day today, consecrated to art.

THE OLD PATRICIAN: According to the calendar?

CAESONIA: No, according to Caligula. He's convoked some poets. He will ask them to improvise a poem on a set theme. And he particularly wants those of you who are poets to take part in the competition. He specially mentioned young Scipio and Metellus.

METELLUS: But we're not ready.

CAESONIA [*in a level tone, as if she has not heard him*]: Needless to say there are prizes. There will be penalties, too. [*Looks of consternation.*] Between ourselves, the penalties won't be so very terrible.

[CALIGULA *enters, looking gloomier than ever.*]

CALIGULA: All ready?

CAESONIA: Yes. [*To a soldier*] Bring in the poets.

[*Enter, two by two, a dozen* POETS, *keeping step; they line up on the right of the stage.*]

CALIGULA: And the others?

CAESONIA: Metellus! Scipio!

[*They cross the stage and take their stand beside the poets.*

CALIGULA *seats himself, back stage on the left, with Caesonia and the Patricians. A short silence.*]

CALIGULA: Subject: Death. Time-limit: one minute.

[*The* POETS *scribble feverishly on their tablets.*]

THE OLD PATRICIAN: Who will compose the jury?

CALIGULA: I. Isn't that enough?

THE OLD PATRICIAN: Oh yes, indeed. Quite enough.

CHEREA: Won't you take part in the competition, Caius?

CALIGULA: Unnecessary. I made my poem on that theme long ago.

THE OLD PATRICIAN [*eagerly*]: Where can one get a copy of it?

CALIGULA: No need to get a copy. I recite it every day, after my fashion.

[CAESONIA *eyes him nervously.* CALIGULA *rounds on her almost savagely.*]

CALIGULA: Is there anything in my appearance that displeases you?

CAESONIA [*gently*]: I'm sorry . . .

CALIGULA: No meekness, please. For heaven's sake, no meekness. You're exasperating enough as it is, but if you start being humble . . .

[CAESONIA *slowly moves away.* CALIGULA *turns to Cherea.*]

CALIGULA: I continue. It's the only poem I have made. And it's proof that I'm the only true artist Rome has known – the only one, believe me – to match his inspiration with his deeds.

CHEREA: That's only a matter of having the power.

CALIGULA: Quite true. Other artists create to compensate for their lack of power. I don't need to make a work of art; I *live* it. [*Roughly*] Well, poets, are you ready?

METELLUS: I think so.

THE OTHERS: Yes.

CALIGULA: Good. Now listen carefully. You are to fall out

of line and come forward one by one. I'll whistle. Number One will start reading his poem. When I whistle, he must stop, and the next begin. And so on. The winner, naturally, will be the one whose poem hasn't been cut short by the whistle. Get ready. [*Turning to Cherea, he whispers*] You see, organization's needed for everything, even for art. [*Blows his whistle.*]

FIRST POET: Death, when beyond thy darkling shore . . .

[*A blast of the whistle. The* POET *steps briskly to the left.* THE OTHERS *will follow the same procedure. These movements should be made with mechanical precision.*]

SECOND POET: In their dim cave, the Fatal Sisters Three . . .

[*Whistle.*]

THIRD POET: Come to me death, beloved . . .

[*A shrill blast of the whistle. The* FOURTH POET *steps forward and strikes a dramatic posture. The whistle goes before he has opened his mouth.*]

FIFTH POET: When I was in my happy infancy . . .

CALIGULA [*yelling*]: Stop that! What earthly connexion has a blockhead's happy infancy with the theme I set? The connexion! Tell me the connexion!

FIFTH POET: But, Caius, I've only just begun, and . . .

[*Shrill blast.*]

SIXTH POET [*in a high-pitched voice*]: Ruthless, he goes his hidden ways . . .

[*Whistle.* SCIPIO *comes forward without a tablet.*]

CALIGULA: You haven't a tablet?

SCIPIO: I do not need one.

CALIGULA: Well, let's hear you. [*He chews at his whistle.*]

SCIPIO [*standing very near Caligula, he recites listlessly, without looking at him*]:

Pursuit of happiness that purifies the heart,
Skies rippling with light,
O wild, sweet, festal joys, frenzy without hope!

CALIGULA [*gently*]: Stop, please. The others needn't compete. [*To Scipio*] You're very young to understand so well the lessons we can learn from Death.

SCIPIO [*gazing straight at Caligula*]: I was very young to lose my father.

CALIGULA [*turning hastily*]: Fall in, the rest of you. No, really a sham poet is too dreadful an infliction. Until now I'd thought of enrolling you as my allies; I sometimes pictured a gallant band of poets defending me in the last ditch. Another illusion gone! I shall have to relegate you to my enemies. So now the poets are against me – and that looks much like the end of all. March out in good order. As you go past you are to lick your tablets so as to efface the atrocities you scrawled on them. Attention! Forward! [*He blows his whistle in short rhythmic jerks.*]

[*Keeping step, the* POETS *file out by the right, tonguing their immortal tablets.*]

CALIGULA [*adds in a lower tone*]: Now leave me, everyone.

[*In the doorway, as they are going out,* CHEREA *touches the First Patrician's shoulder, and speaks in his ear.*]

CHEREA: Now's our opportunity.

[SCIPIO, *who has overheard, halts on the threshold and walks back to Caligula.*]

CALIGULA [*acidly*]: Can't you leave me in peace – as your father's doing?

SCIPIO: No, Caius, all that serves no purpose now. For now I know, I *know* that you have made your choice.

CALIGULA: Won't you leave me in peace!

SCIPIO: Yes, you shall have your wish; I am going to leave you, for I think I've come to understand you. There's no way out left to us, neither to you nor to me – who am like you in so many ways. I shall go away, far away, and try to discover the meaning of it all. [*He gazes at Caligula for some moments. Then, with a rush of emotion*] Good-bye, dear

Caius. When all is ended, remember that I loved you. [*He turns away.*]

[CALIGULA *makes a vague gesture. Then, almost savagely, he pulls himself together and takes some steps towards Caesonia.*]

SCIPIO: You have chosen, Caligula. [*Goes out.*]

CAESONIA: What did he say?

CALIGULA: Nothing you'd understand . . . But come beside me.

[*A short silence.*]

CAESONIA [*nestling against him*]: What are you thinking about?

CALIGULA: I was wondering why I'd kept you with me so long.

CAESONIA: Why, because you're fond of me.

CALIGULA: No. But I think I'd understand – if I had you killed.

CAESONIA: Yes, that would be a solution. Do so, then. . . . But why, oh why can't you relax, if only for a moment, and live freely, without constraint?

CALIGULA: I have been doing that for several years; in fact I've made a practice of it.

CAESONIA: I don't mean that sort of freedom. I mean – Oh, don't you realize what it can be to live and love quite simply, naturally, in . . . in purity of heart?

CALIGULA: This purity of heart you talk of – every man acquires it, in his own way. Mine has been to follow the essential to the end. . . . Still all that needn't prevent me from putting you to death. [*Laughs.*] It would round off my career so well, the perfect climax. [*He rises and swings the mirror round towards himself. Then he walks in a circle, letting his arms hang limp, almost without gestures; there is something feral in his gait, as he continues speaking.*] How strange! When I don't kill, I feel alone. The living don't suffice to people my world and dispel my boredom. I have an impression of an enormous void when you and the others are here, and my eyes see nothing but empty air. No, I'm at ease only in the company of my dead. [*He takes his stand facing the audience, leaning a little forward. He has forgotten Caesonia's presence.*] Only the dead are real. They are of my kind. I see them waiting for me, straining towards me. And I have long talks with this man or that, who screamed to me for mercy and whose tongue I had cut out.

CAESONIA: Come. Lie down beside me. Put your head on my knees.

[CALIGULA *does so.*]

CAESONIA: That's better, isn't it? Now rest. How quiet it is here!

CALIGULA: Quiet? You exaggerate, my dear. Listen! [*Distant metallic tinklings, as of swords or armour.*] Do you hear those thousands of small sounds all around us, hatred stalking its prey? [*Murmuring voices, footsteps.*]

CAESONIA: Nobody would dare . . .

CALIGULA: Yes, stupidity.

CAESONIA: Stupidity doesn't kill. It makes men slow to act.

CALIGULA: It can be murderous, Caesonia. A fool stops at nothing when he thinks his dignity offended. No, it's not the men whose sons or fathers I have killed who'll murder me. *They*, anyhow, have understood. They're with me, they have the same taste in their mouths. But the others – those I made a laughing-stock of – I've no defence against their wounded vanity.

CAESONIA [*passionately*]: We will defend you. There are many of us left who love you.

CALIGULA: Fewer every day. It's not surprising. I've done all that was needed to that end. And then – let's be fair – it's not only stupidity that's against me. There's the courage and the simple faith of men who ask to be happy.

CAESONIA [*in the same tone*]: No, *they* will not kill you. Or, if they tried, fire would come down from heaven and blast them, before they laid a hand on you.

CALIGULA: From heaven! There is no heaven, my poor dear woman! [*He sits down.*] But why this sudden access of devotion? It wasn't catered for in our agreement, if I remember rightly.

CAESONIA [*who has risen from the couch and is pacing the room*]: Don't you understand? Hasn't it been enough to see you killing others, without my also knowing you'll be killed as well? Isn't it enough to feel you hard and cruel, seething with bitterness, when I hold you in my arms; to breathe a reek of murder when you lie on me? Day after day I see all that's human in you dying out, little by little. [*She turns towards him.*] Oh I know. I know I'm getting old, my beauty's on the wane. But it's you only I'm concerned for now; so much so that I've ceased troubling whether you love me. I only want you to get well, quite well again. You're still a boy, really; you've a whole life ahead of you. And, tell me, what greater thing can you want than a whole life?

CALIGULA [*rising, looks at her fixedly*]: You've been with me a long time now, a very long time.

CAESONIA: Yes . . . But you'll keep me, won't you?

CALIGULA: I don't know. I only know that, if you're with me still, it's because of all those nights we've had together, nights of fierce, joyless pleasure; it's because you alone know me as I am. [*He takes her in his arms, bending her head back a little with his right hand.*] I'm twenty-nine. Not a great age really. But today when none the less my life seems so long, so crowded with scraps and shreds of my past selves, so complete in fact, you remain the last witness. And I can't avoid a sort of shameful tenderness for the old woman that you soon will be.

CAESONIA: Tell me that you mean to keep me with you.

CALIGULA: I don't know. All I know – and it's the most terrible thing of all – is that this shameful tenderness is the one sincere emotion that my life has given up to now.

[CAESONIA *frees herself from his arms.* CALIGULA *follows her. She presses her back to his chest and he puts his arms round her.*]

CALIGULA: Wouldn't it be better that the last witness should disappear?

CAESONIA: That has no importance. All I know is: I'm happy. What you've just said has made me very happy. But why can't I share my happiness with you?

CALIGULA: Who says I'm unhappy?

CAESONIA: Happiness is kind. It doesn't thrive on bloodshed.

CALIGULA: Then there must be two kinds of happiness, and I've chosen the murderous kind. For I *am* happy. There was a time when I thought I'd reached the extremity of pain. But, no, one can go farther yet. Beyond the frontier of pain lies a splendid, sterile happiness. Look at me. [*She turns towards him.*] It makes me laugh, Caesonia, when I think how for years and years all Rome carefully avoided uttering Drusilla's name. Well, all Rome was mistaken. Love isn't enough for me; I realized it then. And I realize it again today, when I look at you. To love someone means that one's willing to grow old beside that person. That sort of love is right outside my range. Drusilla old would have been far worse than Drusilla dead. Most people imagine that a man suffers because out of the blue Death snatches away the woman he loves. But his real suffering is less futile; it comes from the discovery that grief, too, cannot last. Even grief is vanity.

You see, I had no excuses, not the shadow of a real love, neither bitterness nor profound regret. Nothing to plead in my defence! But today – you see me still freer than I have been for years; freed as I am from memories and illusion. [*He laughs bitterly.*] I know now that nothing, *nothing* lasts. Think what that knowledge means! There have been just two or three of us in history who really achieved this freedom, this crazy happiness. Well, Caesonia, you have seen out a most unusual drama. It's time the curtain fell, for you. [*He stands behind her, linking his forearm round Caesonia's neck.*]

CAESONIA [*terrified*]: No, it's impossible! How can you call it happiness, this terrifying freedom?

CALIGULA [*gradually tightening his grip on Caesonia's throat*]: Happiness it is, Caesonia; I know what I'm saying. But for this freedom I'd have been a contented man. Thanks to it, I have won the godlike enlightenment of the solitary. [*His exaltation grows as little by little he strangles Caesonia, who puts up no resistance, but holds her hands half-opened, like a suppliant's, before her. Bending his head, he goes on speaking, into her ear.*] I live, I kill, I exercise the rapturous power of a destroyer, compared with which the power of a creator is merest child's-play. And this, *this* is happiness; this and nothing else – this intolerable release, devastating scorn, blood, hatred all around me; the glorious isolation of a man who all his life long nurses and gloats over the joy ineffable of the unpunished murderer; the ruthless logic that crushes out human lives [*he laughs*], that's crushing yours out, Caesonia, so as to perfect at last the utter loneliness that is my heart's desire.

CAESONIA [*struggling feebly*]: Oh, Caius . . .

CALIGULA [*more and more excitedly*]: No. No sentiment. I must have done with it, for the time is short. My time is very short, dear Caesonia. [CAESONIA *is gasping, dying.* CALIGULA *drags her to the bed and lets her fall on it. He stares wildly at her; his voice grows harsh and grating.*] You, too, were guilty. But killing is not the solution. [*He spins round and gazes crazily at the mirror.*] Caligula! You, too; you, too, are guilty. Then what of it – a little more, a little less? Yet who can condemn me in this world where there is no judge, where nobody is innocent? [*He brings his eyes close to his reflected face. He sounds genuinely distressed.*] You see, my poor friend. Helicon has failed you. I shan't have the moon. Never, never, never! But how bitter it is to know all, and to have to go through to the consummation! Listen! That was a sound of weapons. Innocence arming for the fray – and innocence will triumph. Why am I not in their place, amongst them? And I'm afraid. That's cruellest of all, after despising others, to find oneself as cowardly as they. Still, no matter. Fear, too, has an end. Soon I shall attain that emptiness beyond all understanding, in which the heart has rest. [*He steps back a few paces, then returns to the mirror. He seems calmer. When he speaks again his voice is steadier, less shrill.*]

Yet, really, it's quite simple. If I'd had the moon, if love were enough, all might have been different. But where could I quench this thirst? What human heart, what god, would have for me the depth of a great lake? [*Kneeling, weeping*] There's nothing in this world, or in the other, made to my stature. And yet I know, and you too know [*still weeping, he stretches out his arms towards the mirror*] that all I need is for the impossible to be. The impossible! I've searched for it at the confines of the world, in the secret places of my heart. I've stretched out my hands; [*his voice rises to a scream*] see, I stretch out my hands, but it's always you I find, you only, confronting me, and I've come to hate you. I have chosen a wrong path, a path that leads to nothing. My freedom isn't the right one . . . Nothing, nothing yet. Oh, how oppressive is this darkness! Helicon has not come; we shall be for ever guilty.

CALIGULA

The air tonight is heavy as the sum of human sorrows. [*A clash of arms and whisperings are heard in the wings.* CALIGULA *rises, picks up a stool and returns to the mirror, breathing heavily. He contemplates himself, makes a slight leap forward and, watching the symmetrical movement of his reflected self, hurls the stool at it, screaming*] To history, Caligula! Go down to history! [*The mirror breaks and at the same moment armed conspirators rush in.* CALIGULA *swings round to face them, with a mad laugh.* SCIPIO *and* CHEREA, *who are in front, fling themselves at him and stab his face with their daggers.* CALIGULA'S *laughter turns to gasps. All strike him, hurriedly, confusedly. In a last gasp, laughing and choking,* CALIGULA *shrieks*] I'm still alive!

CURTAIN

CROSS PURPOSE

A Play in Three Acts

Characters

THE OLD MANSERVANT, *no determinate age*
MARTHA, *the sister, aged thirty*
THE MOTHER, *aged sixty*
JAN, *the son, aged thirty-eight*
MARIA, *his wife, aged thirty*

ACT ONE

Noon. The inn-parlour; a clean, brightly lit room. Everything is very spick and span.

THE MOTHER: He'll come back.

MARTHA: Did he tell you so?

THE MOTHER: Yes.

MARTHA: Alone?

THE MOTHER: That I can't say.

MARTHA: He doesn't look like a poor man.

THE MOTHER: No, and he never asked what our charges were.

MARTHA: A good sign, that. But usually rich men don't travel alone. Really it's *that* makes things so difficult. You may have to wait ages when you're looking out for a man who is not only rich but quite alone.

THE MOTHER: Yes, we don't get so many opportunities.

MARTHA: It means, of course, that we've had many slack times these last few years. This place is often empty. Poor folks who stop here never stay long, and it's mighty seldom rich ones come.

THE MOTHER: Don't grumble about that, Martha. Rich people give a lot of extra work.

MARTHA [*looking hard at her*]: But they pay well. [*A short silence.*] Tell me, mother; what's come over you? For some time I've noticed that you weren't quite . . . quite your usual self.

THE MOTHER: I'm tired, my dear, that's all. What I need is a long rest.

MARTHA: Listen, mother. I can take over the household

work you're doing now. Then you'll have your days free.

THE MOTHER: That wasn't quite the sort of rest I meant. Oh, I suppose it's just an old woman's fancy. All I'm longing for is peace – to be able to relax a little. [*She gives a little laugh.*] I know it sounds silly, Martha, but some evenings I feel almost like taking to religion.

MARTHA: You're not so very old, mother; you haven't come to that yet. And, anyhow, I should say *you* could do better.

THE MOTHER: Of course I was only joking, my dear. All the same . . . at the end of one's life, it's not a bad idea to take things easy. One can't be always on the stretch, as you are, Martha. And it isn't natural for a woman of your age, either. I know plenty of girls who were born the same year as you, and they think only of pleasure and excitements.

MARTHA: Their pleasures and excitements are nothing compared to ours, don't you agree, mother?

THE MOTHER: I'd rather you didn't speak of that.

MARTHA [*thoughtfully*]: Really one would think that nowadays some words burn your tongue.

THE MOTHER: What can it matter to you – provided I don't shrink from acts? But that has no great importance. What I really meant was that I'd like to see you smile now and again.

MARTHA: I do smile sometimes, I assure you.

THE MOTHER: Really? I've never seen you.

MARTHA: That's because I smile when I'm by myself, in my bedroom.

THE MOTHER [*looking closely at her*]: What a hard face you have, Martha!

MARTHA [*coming closer; calmly*]: Ah, so you don't approve of my face?

THE MOTHER [*after a short silence, still looking at her*]: I wonder . . . Yes, I think I do.

MARTHA [*emotionally*]: Oh, mother, can't you understand? Once we have enough money in hand, and I can escape from this shut-in valley; once we can say good-bye to this inn and this dreary town where it's always raining; once we've forgotten this land of shadows – ah then, when my dream has come true, and we're living beside the sea, *then* you will see me smile. Unhappily one needs a great deal of money to be able to live in freedom by the sea. That is why we mustn't be afraid of words; that is why we must take trouble over this man who's come to stay here. If he is rich enough, perhaps my freedom will begin with him.

THE MOTHER: If he's rich enough, and if he's by himself.

MARTHA: That's so. He has to be by himself as well. Did he talk much to you, mother?

THE MOTHER: No, he said very little.

MARTHA: When he asked for his room, did you notice how he looked?

THE MOTHER: No. My sight's none too good, as you know, and I didn't really look at his face. I've learnt from experience that it's better not to look at them too closely. It's easier to kill what one doesn't know. [*A short silence.*] There! That should please you. You can't say now that I'm afraid of words.

MARTHA: Yes, and I prefer it so. I've no use for hints and evasions. Crime is crime, and one should know what one is about. And, from what you've just said, it looks as if you had it in mind when you were talking to that traveller.

THE MOTHER: No, I wouldn't say I had it in mind – it was more from force of habit.

MARTHA: Habit? But you said yourself that these opportunities seldom come our way.

THE MOTHER: Certainly. But habit begins with the second crime. With the first nothing starts, but something ends. Then, too, while we have had few opportunities, they have been spread out over many years, and memory helps to build up habits. Yes, it was force of habit that made me keep my eyes off that man when I was talking to him and, all the same, convinced me he had the look of a victim.

MARTHA: Mother, we must kill him.

THE MOTHER [*in a low tone*]: Eh, yes, I suppose we'll have to.

MARTHA: You said that in a curious way.

THE MOTHER: I'm tired, that's a fact. Anyhow, I'd like this one to be the last. It's terribly tiring to kill. And, though really I care little where I die – beside the sea or here, far inland – I do hope we will get away together, the moment it's over.

MARTHA: Indeed we shall – and what a glorious moment that will be! So, cheer up, mother, there won't be much to do. You know quite well there's no question of killing. He'll drink his tea, he'll go to sleep, and he'll be still alive when we carry him to the river. Some day, long after, he will be found jammed against the weir, along with others who didn't have his luck and threw themselves into the water with their eyes open. Do you remember last year when we were watching them repair the sluices, how you said that our ones suffered least, and life was crueller than we? So don't lose heart, you'll be having your rest quite soon and I'll be seeing what I've never seen.

THE MOTHER: Yes, Martha, I won't lose heart. And it was quite true, what you said about 'our ones'. I'm always glad to think they never suffered. Really, it's hardly a crime, only a sort of intervention, a flick of the finger given to unknown lives. And it's also quite true that, by the look of it, life is crueller than we. Perhaps that is why I can't manage to feel guilty. I can only just manage to feel tired.

[*The old* MANSERVANT *comes in. He seats himself behind the bar counter and remains there, neither moving nor speaking, until* JAN'S *entrance.*]

MARTHA: Which room shall we put him in?

THE MOTHER: Any room, provided it's on the first floor.

MARTHA: Yes, we had a lot of needless trouble last time, with the two flights of stairs. [*For the first time she sits down.*] Tell me, mother, is it true that down on the coast the sand's so hot it scorches one's feet?

THE MOTHER: As you know, Martha, I've never been there. But I've been told the sun burns everything up.

MARTHA: I read in a book that it even burns out people's souls and gives them bodies that shine like gold but are quite hollow, there's nothing left inside.

THE MOTHER: Is that what makes you want to go there so much?

MARTHA: Yes, my soul's a burden to me, I've had enough of it. I'm eager to be in that country, where the sun kills every question. I don't belong here.

THE MOTHER: Unfortunately we have much to do beforehand. Of course, when it's over, I'll go there with you. But I am not like you; I shall not have the feeling of going to a place where I belong. After a certain age one knows there is no resting-place anywhere. Indeed there's something to be said for this ugly brick house we've made our home and stocked with memories; there are times when one can fall asleep in it. But, naturally it would mean something, too, if I could have sleep and forgetfulness together. [*She rises and walks towards the door.*] Well, Martha, get everything ready. [*Pauses.*] If it's really worth the effort.

[MARTHA *watches her go out. Then she, too, leaves by another door. For some moments only the old* MANSERVANT *is on the stage.* JAN *enters, stops, glances round the room and sees the old man sitting behind the counter.*]

JAN: Nobody about? [*The old man gazes at him, rises, crosses the stage and goes out.* MARIA *enters.* JAN *swings round on her.*] So you followed me!

MARIA: Forgive me – I couldn't help it. I may not stay long. Only please let me look at the place where I'm leaving you.

JAN: Somebody may come, and your being here will upset all my plans.

MARIA: Do please let us take the chance of someone's coming and my telling who you are. I know you don't want it, but – [*He turns away fretfully. A short silence.* MARIA *is examining the room.*] So this is the place?

JAN: Yes. That's the door I went out by, twenty years ago. My sister was a little girl. She was playing in that corner. My mother didn't come to kiss me. At the time I thought I didn't care.

MARIA: Jan, I can't believe they failed to recognize you just now. A mother's bound to recognize her son; it's the least she can do.

JAN: Perhaps. Still, twenty years' separation makes a difference. Life has been going on since I left. My mother's grown old, her sight is failing. I hardly recognized her myself.

MARIA [*impatiently*]: I know. You came in; you said 'Good day'; you sat down. This room wasn't like the one you remembered.

JAN: Yes, my memory had played me false. They received me without a word. I was given the glass of beer I asked for. I was looked at, but I wasn't *seen*. Everything was more difficult than I'd expected.

MARIA: You know quite well it needn't have been difficult; you had only to speak. On such occasions one says 'It's I' and then it's all plain sailing.

JAN: True. But I'd been imagining – all sorts of things. I'd expected a welcome like the prodigal son's. Actually I was given a glass of beer, against payment. It took the words out of my mouth, and I thought I'd better let things take their course.

MARIA: There was nothing to take its course. It was another of those ideas of yours – and a word would have been enough.

JAN: It wasn't an idea of mine, Maria; it was the force of things. What's more, I'm not in such a hurry. I have come here to bring them my money and, if I can, some happiness. When I learnt about my father's death I realized I had duties towards these two women and now, as a result, I'm doing what it's right for me to do. But evidently it is not so easy as people think, coming back to one's old home, and it takes time to change a stranger into a son.

MARIA: But why not let them know the truth at once? There are situations in which the normal way of acting is obviously the best. If one wants to be recognized, one starts by telling one's name; that's common sense. Otherwise, by pretending to be what one is not, one simply muddles everything. How could you expect not to be treated as a stranger in a house you entered under false colours? No, dear, there's something . . . something morbid about the way you're going on.

JAN: Oh come, Maria! It's not so serious as that. And, mind you, it suits my plan. I shall take this opportunity of seeing them from the outside. Then I'll have a better notion of what to do to make them happy. Afterwards, I'll find some way of getting them to recognize me. It's just a matter of choosing one's words.

MARIA: No, there's only one way, and it's to do what any ordinary mortal would do – to say, 'It's I,' and to let one's heart speak for itself.

JAN: The heart isn't so simple as all that.

MARIA: But it uses simple words. Surely there was no difficulty in saying, 'I'm your son. This is my wife. I've been living with her in a country we both love, a land of endless sunshine beside the sea. But something was lacking there, to complete my happiness, and now I feel I need you.'

JAN: Don't be unfair, Maria. I don't need them; but I realized they may need me, and a man doesn't live only for himself.

[*A short silence.* MARIA *looks away from him.*]

MARIA: Perhaps you are right. I'm sorry for what I said. But I have grown terribly suspicious since coming to this country where I've looked in vain for a single happy face. This Europe of yours is so sad. Since we've been here, I haven't once heard you laugh and, personally, I feel my nerves on edge all the time. Oh, why did you make me leave my country? Let's go away, Jan; we shall not find happiness here.

JAN: It's not happiness we've come for. We had happiness already.

MARIA [*passionately*]: Then why not have been satisfied with it?

JAN: Happiness isn't everything; there is duty, too. Mine was to come back to my mother and my own country. [MARIA *makes a protesting gesture and is about to answer.* JAN *checks her. Footsteps can be heard.*] Someone's coming. Do please go, Maria.

MARIA: No, I can't, I can't! Not yet, anyhow!

JAN [*as the footsteps approach*]: Go there. [*He gently pushes her towards the door at the back. The old* MANSERVANT *crosses the room without seeing Maria, and goes out by the other door.*] Now, leave at once. You see, luck is on my side.

MARIA: Do, please, let me stay. I promise not to speak a word, only to stay beside you till you're recognized.

JAN: No. You'd give me away.

[*She turns away, then comes back and looks him in the eyes.*]

MARIA: Jan, we've been married for five years.

JAN: Yes, almost five years.

MARIA [*lowering her eyes*]: And this will be the first night we spend apart. [*He says nothing and she looks up, gazing earnestly at him.*] I've always loved everything about you, even what I didn't understand, and I know that really I wouldn't wish you to be other than you are. I'm not a very troublesome wife, am I? But here I'm scared of the empty bed you are sending me to, and I'm afraid, too, of your forsaking me.

JAN: Surely you can trust my love better than that?

MARIA: I do trust it. But besides your love there are your dreams – or your duties; they're the same thing. They take you away from me so often, and at those moments it's as if you were having a holiday from me. But I can't take a holiday from you, and tonight [*she presses herself to him, weeping*], this night without you – oh, I shall never be able to bear it!

JAN [*clasping her tightly*]: But this is childishness, my dear!

MARIA: Of course it's childish. But . . . but we were so happy over there, and it's not my fault if the nights in this country terrify me. I don't want to be alone tonight.

JAN: But do try to understand, my dear; I've a promise to keep, and it's most important.

MARIA: What promise?

JAN: The one I made to myself on the day I understood my mother needed me.

MARIA: You've another promise to keep.

JAN: Yes?

MARIA: The promise you made me on the day you joined your life to mine.

JAN: But surely I can keep both promises. What I'm asking of you is nothing very terrible. Nor is it a mere caprice. Only one evening and one night in which to take my bearings here, get to know better these two women who are dear to me, and to secure their happiness.

MARIA [*shaking her head*]: A separation always means a lot to people who love each other – with the right kind of love.

JAN: But, you romantic little creature, you know quite well I love you with the right kind of love.

MARIA: No, Jan. Men do not know how real love should be. Nothing they have can ever satisfy them. They're always dreaming dreams, building up new duties, going to new countries and new homes. Women are different; they know that life is short and one must make haste to love, to share the same bed, embrace the man one loves, and dread every separation. When one loves one has no time for dreams.

JAN: But, really, dear, aren't you exaggerating? It's such a simple thing I'm doing; trying to get in touch again with my mother, to help her and bring her happiness. As for my dreams and duties, you'll have to take them as they are. Without them I'd be a mere shadow of myself; indeed you'd love me less, were I without them.

MARIA [*turning her back to him abruptly*]: Oh, I know you can talk me round, you can always find good reasons for anything you want to do. But I refuse to listen, I stop my ears when you start speaking in that special voice I know so well. It's the voice of your loneliness, not of love.

JAN [*standing behind her*]: Don't let's talk of that now, Maria.

All I'm asking is to be left here by myself, so that I can clear up certain things in my mind. Really it's nothing so very terrible, or extraordinary, my sleeping under the same roof as my mother. God will see to the rest and He knows, too, that in acting thus I'm not forgetting you. Only – no one can be happy in exile or estrangement. One can't remain a stranger all one's life. It is quite true that a man needs happiness, but he also needs to find his true place in the world. And I believe that coming back to my country, making the happiness of those I love, will help me to do this. I don't look any farther.

MARIA: Surely you could do it without all these . . . these complications? No, Jan, I'm afraid you are going the wrong way about it.

JAN: It's the right way, because it's the only way of finding out whether or not I did well to have those 'dreams'.

MARIA: I hope you'll find that you did well. Personally, I have only one dream – of that country where we were happy together; and only one duty – towards you.

JAN [*embracing her*]: Let me have my way, dear. I'll find the things to say that will put everything right.

MARIA [*in an access of emotion*]: Then follow your dream, dear. Nothing matters, if only I keep your love. Usually I can't be unhappy when you hold me in your arms. I bide my time, I wait till you come down from the clouds; and then my hour begins. What makes me so unhappy today is that, though I'm quite sure of your love, I'm no less sure you will not let me stay with you. That's why men's love is so cruel, so heart-rending. They can't prevent themselves from leaving what they value most.

JAN [*holding her face between his hands, and smiling*]: Quite true, my dear. But come now! Look at me! I'm not in any danger, as you seem to fear. I'm carrying out my plan, and I know all will be well. You're entrusting me for just one night to my mother and my sister; there's nothing so alarming about that, is there?

MARIA [*freeing herself*]: Then – good-bye! And may my love shield you from harm. [*She goes to the door, and holds out her hands.*] See how poor I am; they're empty! You – you're going forward to adventure. I can only wait. [*After a momentary hesitation she goes out.*]

[JAN *sits down.* MARTHA *enters.*]

JAN: Good afternoon. I've come about the room.

MARTHA: I know. It's being got ready. But, first, I must enter you in our Visitors' Book. [*She goes out and comes back with the register.*]

JAN: I must say, your servant is a very queer fellow.

MARTHA: This is the first time we've had any complaint about him. He always carries out his duties quite satisfactorily.

JAN: Oh, I wasn't complaining. I only meant that he seemed a bit of a character. Is he dumb?

MARTHA: It's not that.

JAN: Ah! then he does speak.

MARTHA: As little as possible and only when really necessary.

JAN: Anyhow, he doesn't seem to hear what one says.

MARTHA: It's not so much that he doesn't hear; only he hears badly. Now I must ask you for your name and Christian names.

JAN: Hasek, Karl.

MARTHA: Only Karl?

JAN: Yes.

MARTHA: Date and place of birth?

JAN: I'm thirty-eight.

MARTHA: Yes, but where were you born?

JAN [*after a brief hesitation*]: Oh, in . . . in Bohemia.

MARTHA: Profession?

JAN: None.

MARTHA: One has to be very rich, or very poor, to travel, when one does no work.

JAN [*smiling*]: I'm not very poor and, for several reasons, I'm glad it's so.

MARTHA [*in a different tone*]: You're a Czech, I suppose?

JAN: Certainly.

MARTHA: Your usual residence?

JAN: In Bohemia.

MARTHA: Have you come from there?

JAN: No, I've come from the south. [*She looks at him questioningly.*] From across the sea.

MARTHA: Ah, yes. [*A short silence.*] Do you go there often?

JAN: Fairly often.

MARTHA [*she seems lost in thought for some moments before continuing*]: And where are you going?

JAN: I've not decided. It will depend on a lot of things.

MARTHA: Then do you propose to stay here?

JAN: I don't know. It depends on what I find here.

MARTHA: That doesn't matter. Is no one here expecting you?

JAN: No, I couldn't say anyone's expecting me.

MARTHA: You have your identity papers, I suppose?

JAN: Yes, I can show you them.

MARTHA: Don't trouble. I've only got to write down whether you have an identity card or a passport.

JAN [*producing a passport from his pocket*]: I've a passport. Here it is. Will you have a look at it?

[*She takes it, but her thoughts are obviously elsewhere. She seems to be weighing it in her palm; then she hands it back.*]

MARTHA: No, keep it. When you're over there, do you live near the sea?

JAN: Yes.

[*She gets up, seems about to put the book away; then, changing her mind, holds it open in front of her.*]

MARTHA [*with sudden harshness*]: Ah, I was forgetting. Have you a family?

JAN: Well, I had one once. But I left them many years ago.

MARTHA: No, I meant, are you married?

JAN: Why do you ask that? I've never had the question put to me in any other hotel.

MARTHA: It's one of the questions on the list given us by the police.

JAN: You surprise me . . . Yes, I'm married. Didn't you notice my wedding ring?

MARTHA: No, I didn't. It's none of my business to look at your hands; I'm here to fill in your registration form. Your wife's address, please.

JAN: Well, she . . . as a matter of fact, she's stayed behind, in her country.

MARTHA: Ah! Very good. [*Closes the book.*] Shall I bring you a drink now, while your room's being got ready?

JAN: No, thanks. But, if you don't mind, I'll stay here. I hope I shan't be in your way.

MARTHA: Why should you be in my way? This is a public room, for the use of our customers.

JAN: Quite so. But someone by himself can be more of a nuisance than a crowd of people.

MARTHA: Why? I presume you don't intend to waste my time with idle chatter. I've no use for folks who come here and try to play the fool – and you should have guessed that. The people hereabouts have learnt it, anyhow, and you'll very soon see for yourself that this is a quiet inn, and you'll have all the calm you want. Hardly anybody comes here.

JAN: That can't be very good for business.

MARTHA: We may lose some takings, but we make up for them in peace, and peace is something for which you can't pay too high a price. And don't forget that one good customer is better than a roaring trade; so that's what we are out for – the right kind of visitor.

JAN: But . . . [*He hesitates.*] Isn't your life here a bit dull at times? Don't you and your mother find it very lonely?

MARTHA [*rounding on him angrily*]: I decline to answer such questions. You had no business to ask them, and you should have known it. I can see I'll have to warn you how things stand. As a guest at this inn you have the rights and privileges of a guest, but nothing more. Still, don't be afraid, you will have every attention you're entitled to. You will be very well looked after and I shall be greatly surprised if ever you complain of your reception here. But I fail to see why we should go out of our way to give you special reasons for satisfaction. That's why your questions are out of place. It has nothing to do with you whether or not we feel lonely; just as you need not trouble yourself whether you cause us inconvenience or ask too much of us. By all means stand upon your rights as a guest. But do not go beyond them.

JAN: I beg your pardon. Nothing was further from my intention than to offend you; I only wanted to show my good will. I had a feeling that perhaps we weren't quite so remote from each other as you seem to think; no more than that.

MARTHA: I can see I must repeat what I was saying. There can be no question of offending me or not offending me. Since you seem determined to adopt an attitude which you have no right to adopt, I prefer to make things clear. I can assure you I'm not in the least vexed. Only it is in our interest, yours and mine, that we should keep our distance. If you persist in talking in a manner unbecoming a guest, there's no alternative; we must refuse to have you here. But if you will understand, as I cannot doubt you will, that two women who let you a room in their hotel are under no obligation to treat you as a friend into the bargain, all will go smoothly.

JAN: I quite agree; and it was inexcusable, my giving you an impression that I failed to understand this.

MARTHA: Oh, there's no great harm done. You are not the first who's tried to take that line. But I always made it pretty clear how we felt about such matters, and that settled it.

JAN: Yes, you certainly have made it clear, and I suppose I'd better say no more – for the present.

MARTHA: Not at all. There's nothing to prevent your talking as a guest should talk.

JAN: And how should a guest talk?

MARTHA: Most of our guests talk about all sorts of things: politics, their travels, and so forth. Never about my mother or myself – and that is as it should be. Some of them even talk about their private lives or their jobs. And that, too, is within their rights. After all, one of the services for which we're paid is listening to our customers. But it goes without saying that the charges made for board and lodging don't oblige hotel keepers to answer personal questions. My mother may do so sometimes, out of indifference; but I make a principle of refusing. Once you've grasped this, we shall not only be on excellent terms, but you'll discover you have many things to tell us, and that sometimes it's quite pleasant to be listened to when one's talking about oneself.

JAN: I'm afraid you won't find me much good at talking about myself. But, really, that won't be necessary. If I stay here only a short time, there will be no point in your getting to know me. And if I make a long stay, you'll have plenty of opportunity of knowing who I am, without my speaking.

MARTHA: I hope that you will not bear me any malice for

what I've told you. There'd be no reason for it, anyhow. I've always found it better to be quite frank, and I had to stop your talking in a tone that was bound to lead to strained relations. Really I'm asking nothing out-of-the-way. Until today there was nothing in common between us, and some very special reasons would be needed for our suddenly becoming intimate. And you must forgive me if I fail to see, so far, anything in the least resembling a reason of that kind.

JAN: I'd forgiven you already. Indeed, I quite agree that intimacy isn't come by at a moment's notice; one has to earn it. So if you now consider that everything's been cleared up between us, I can only say I'm very glad of it.

[THE MOTHER *enters.*]

THE MOTHER: Good afternoon, sir. Your room is ready now.

JAN: Thanks very much, madame.

[THE MOTHER *sits down.*]

THE MOTHER [*to Martha*]: Have you filled in the form?

MARTHA: Yes, I've done that.

THE MOTHER: May I have a look? You must excuse me, sir, but the police here are very strict. . . . Yes, I see my daughter's not put down whether you've come here on business, or for reasons of health, or as a tourist.

JAN: Well, let's say as a tourist.

THE MOTHER: To see the Monastery, no doubt? It's thought very highly of, I'm told.

JAN: Yes, indeed; I've heard a lot about it. Also I wanted to see this place again. It has very pleasant memories for me.

THE MOTHER: Did you ever live here?

JAN: No, but a long time ago I happened to come this way, and I've never forgotten that visit.

THE MOTHER: Still, this is just an ordinary little country town.

JAN: That's so. But I'm much attached to it. Indeed, ever since I came here I've been feeling almost at home.

THE MOTHER: Will you be staying long?

JAN: Really I don't know. I dare say that surprises you, but it's the truth. I don't know. To stay in a place you need to have reasons – friendships, the presence of people you are fond of. Otherwise there'd be no point in staying there rather than elsewhere. And since it's hard to know if one will be made welcome, it's natural for me to be uncertain about my plans.

THE MOTHER: That sounds a little vague, if I may say so.

JAN: I know, but I can't express myself better, I'm afraid.

THE MOTHER: Anyhow, I expect you'll soon have had enough of this place.

JAN: No, I've a faithful heart, and I soon build up memories and attachments, if I'm given a chance.

MARTHA [*impatiently*]: A faithful heart, indeed! Hearts count for mighty little here!

JAN [*seeming not to have heard her; to the Mother*]: You seem terribly disillusioned. Have you been living long in this hotel?

THE MOTHER: For years and years. So many years that I have quite forgotten when it began and the woman I was then. This girl is my daughter. She's kept beside me all through those years, and probably that's why I know she is my daughter. Otherwise I might have forgotten her, too.

MARTHA: Really, mother! You've no reason to tell him all that.

THE MOTHER: You're right, Martha.

JAN [*hastily*]: Please don't say any more. But how well I understand your feelings, madame; they're what one comes to at the end of a long, hard-working life. Yet perhaps it might have been quite different if you'd been helped, as every woman should be helped, and given the support of a man's arm.

THE MOTHER: Oh, once upon a time I had it – but there was too much work to do. My husband and I, together, could hardly cope with it. We hadn't even time to think of each other; I believe I had forgotten him even before he died.

JAN: That, too, I can understand. But [*he hesitates for a moment*] – perhaps if a son had been here to give you a helping hand, you wouldn't have forgotten *him*?

MARTHA: Mother, you know we've a lot of work to do.

THE MOTHER: A son? Oh, I'm too old, too old! Old women forget to love even their sons. Hearts wear out, sir.

JAN: That's so. But he, I'm sure, doesn't forget.

MARTHA [*standing between them; peremptorily*]: If a son came here, he'd find exactly what an ordinary guest can count on: amiable indifference, no more and no less. All the men we have had here received that, and it satisfied them. They paid for their rooms and were given a key. They didn't talk about their hearts. [*A short silence.*] That simplified our work.

THE MOTHER: Don't talk about that.

JAN [*reflectively*]: Did they stay here long?

MARTHA: Some of them, a very long time. We did all that was needed for them to stay. Those who weren't so well off left after the first night. We didn't do anything for them.

JAN: I've plenty of money and I propose to stay some little time in this hotel – if you're willing to keep me. I forgot to mention that I can pay you in advance.

THE MOTHER: Oh, we never ask people to do that.

MARTHA: If you are rich, so much the better. But no more talk about your heart, please. We can do nothing about that. In fact your way of speaking got so much on my nerves that I very nearly asked you to go. Take your key and make yourself comfortable in your room. But remember you are in a house where the heart isn't catered for. Too many bleak years have passed over this little spot of Central Europe, and they've drained all the warmth out of this house. They have killed any desire for friendliness and, let me repeat it, you won't find anything in the least like intimacy here. You will get what the few travellers who lodge with us are used to get, and it has nothing to do with sentiment. So take your key and bear this well in mind: we're accepting you as a guest, in our quiet way, for interested motives, and if we keep you it will be in our quiet way, for interested motives.

[JAN *takes the key and watches her go out.*]

THE MOTHER: Don't pay too much attention to what she says. But it's a fact there's some things she never could bear talking about. [*She starts to rise. He comes forward to help her.*] Don't trouble, my son; I'm not a cripple yet. Look at my hands; they're still quite strong. Strong enough to hold up a man's legs. [*A short silence. He is gazing at the key.*] Is it what I just said that you're thinking about?

JAN: No. I'm sorry, I hardly heard it. But, tell me, why did you say 'my son' just now?

THE MOTHER: Oh, I shouldn't have done that, sir. I didn't mean to take liberties. It was just . . . a manner of speaking.

JAN: I quite understand. Now I'll have a look at my room.

THE MOTHER: Certainly, sir. Our old manservant is waiting for you in the passage. [*He gazes at her, on the brink of speaking.*] Is there anything you want?

JAN [*hesitantly*]: Well . . . no, madame. Except that I'd like to thank you for your welcome. [*He goes out.*]

[*Left to herself,* THE MOTHER *sits down again, lays her hands on the table, and contemplates them.*]

THE MOTHER: That was a queer thing I did just now, talking about my hands. Still, if he had really looked at them, perhaps he'd have guessed what he refused to understand in Martha's words. But why must this man be so much bent on dying, and I so little on killing? If only he'd leave – then I could have another long night's rest! I'm too old. Too old to lock my hands again on a man's ankles and feel the body swaying, swaying, all the way down to the river. Too old for that last effort when we launch him into the water. It will leave me gasping for breath, and every muscle aching, with my arms hanging limp, without even the strength to wipe off the drops that splash up when the sleeping body plunges into the eddies. Too old, too old! . . . Well, well, since I must, I must! He is the perfect victim and it's for me to give him the sleep I wanted for my own night. And so . . .

[MARTHA *enters abruptly.*]

MARTHA: There you are, day-dreaming again! And yet – we've much to do.

THE MOTHER: I was thinking of that man. No, really I was thinking of myself.

MARTHA: You'd do better to think about tomorrow. What good was it, not looking at that man, if you can't keep your thoughts off him? You said yourself, it's easier to kill what one doesn't know. Do be *sensible.*

THE MOTHER: That was one of your father's favourite words, I remember. But I'd like to feel sure this is the last time we'll have to be . . . sensible. It's odd. When your father used that word it was to drive away the fear of being found out, but when you tell me to be sensible it's only to quench the little spark of goodness that was kindling in my heart.

MARTHA: What you call a spark of goodness is merely sleepiness. But, only postpone your languor till tomorrow, and then you'll be able to take things easy for the rest of your days.

THE MOTHER: You're right, I know. But why should chance have sent us a victim who is so . . . so unsuitable?

MARTHA: Chance doesn't enter into it. But I admit this traveller is really too confiding, his innocence is too much of a good thing. What would the world come to if condemned men started unbosoming their sentimental troubles to the hangman? It's unsound in principle. But it aggravates me too, and when I'm dealing with him, I'll bring to bear some of the anger I always feel at the stupidity of men.

THE MOTHER: That, too, is unsound. In the past we brought neither anger nor pity to our task; only the indifference it needed. But tonight I am tired, and you, I see, are angered. Are we really obliged to go through with it under these conditions, and to override everything for the sake of a little more money?

MARTHA: Not for money, but for a home beside the sea, and forgetfulness of this hateful country. You may be tired of living, but I, too, am tired, tired to death of these narrow horizons. I feel I couldn't endure another month here. Both of us are sick of this inn and everything to do with it. You, who are old, want no more than to shut your eyes and to forget. But I can still feel in my heart some of the absurd desires I had when I was twenty, and I want to act in such a way as to have done with them for ever – even if, for that, we must go a little further with the life we want to leave. And really it's your duty to help me; it was you who brought me into the world in a land of clouds and mist, instead of a land of sunshine.

THE MOTHER: Martha, I almost wonder if it wouldn't be better for me to be forgotten, as I've been forgotten by your brother, than to hear you speaking to me in that tone, the tone of an accuser.

MARTHA: You know well I did not mean to wound you. [*A short silence; then passionately*] What could I do without you? What would become of me if you were far away? I, anyhow, could never, never forget you, and if at times the strain of this life we lead makes me fail in the respect I owe you, I beg you, mother, to forgive me.

THE MOTHER: You are a good daughter, Martha, and I can well believe that an old woman is sometimes hard to understand. But, I feel this is the moment to tell you what I've been trying all this time to say: 'Not tonight.'

MARTHA: What! Are we to wait till tomorrow? You know quite well you've never had such an idea before; and it would never do for him to have time to meet people here. No, we must act while we have him to ourselves.

THE MOTHER: Perhaps. I don't know. But not tonight. Let him be for this one night. It will give us a reprieve; we shall breathe freely for a while and enjoy the little lull of peace that comes, they say, at the heart of the worst crimes. Yes, let us have this respite. And perhaps it's through him we shall save ourselves.

MARTHA: Save ourselves? Why should we want to do that, and what an absurd thing to say! All you can hope for is to gain by what you do tonight the right to sleep your fill, once it's over.

THE MOTHER: That's what I meant by 'saving ourselves'. To retain the hope of sleep.

MARTHA: Good! Then I swear it's in our hands to work out our salvation. Mother, we must have done with indecision. Tonight it shall be; or not at all.

CURTAIN

ACT TWO

A bedroom at the inn. Dusk is falling. JAN *is gazing out of the window.*

JAN: Maria was right. This evening hour tells on the nerves. [*A short pause.*] I wonder what her thoughts are, what she is up to, in that other hotel bedroom. I picture her huddled up in a chair; she's not crying, but her heart's like ice. Over there the nightfall brought a promise of happiness. But here . . . [*Looks round the room.*] Nonsense! I've no reason for feeling this uneasiness. When a man starts something, he has no business to look back. It's in this room everything will be settled.

[*A sharp rap on the door.* MARTHA *comes in.*]

MARTHA: I hope I'm not disturbing you. I only wanted to change the towels and fill your jug.

JAN: Oh, I thought it had been done.

MARTHA: No. The old man who works for us sometimes forgets things like that.

JAN: They're only details, anyhow. . . . But I hardly dare to tell you that you're not disturbing me.

MARTHA: Why?

JAN: I'm not sure that's allowed for in our . . . our agreement.

MARTHA: You see! You can't answer like any ordinary person, even when you want to make things easy.

JAN [*smiling*]: Sorry. I shall have to train myself. Only you must give me a little time.

MARTHA [*busy with the room*]: Yes, that's the whole point.

[*He turns and looks out of the window. She studies him. His back is to her. She continues speaking as she works.*] I'm sorry, sir, that this room is not as comfortable as you might wish.

JAN: It's spotlessly clean, and that is something one appreciates. Unless I'm much mistaken, you had it done up not very long ago.

MARTHA: Quite true. But how can you tell that?

JAN: Oh, by some details.

MARTHA: Anyhow, many of our guests grumble because there isn't running water, and I can hardly blame them. Also, there should be a lamp above the bed; for some time we've been meaning to have one installed. It must be rather a nuisance for people who're used to reading in bed to have to get up to switch the light off.

JAN [*turning towards her*]: That's so. I hadn't noticed. Still it's not a very serious drawback.

MARTHA: It's kind of you to take it like that. I am glad the defects of our hotel don't trouble you; in fact you seem to notice them less than we do. I've known people whom they'd have been enough to drive away.

JAN: I hope you'll let me make a remark that goes beyond our pact – and say that you're a very surprising person. One certainly doesn't expect hotel-keepers to go out of their way to point out defects in the accommodation. Really it almost looks as if you wanted to make me leave.

MARTHA: That wasn't quite what I had in mind. [*Coming to a sudden decision*] But it's a fact that mother and I are rather reluctant to have you here.

JAN: I must say I noticed that you weren't doing much to keep me. Still, I can't imagine why. You have no reason to doubt my solvency, and I hardly think I give the impression of someone with a crime on his conscience.

MARTHA: Certainly not. If you must know, not only don't you look in the least like a criminal, but you produce the opposite effect – of complete innocence. Our reasons were quite different from what you think. We intend to leave this hotel shortly and we've been meaning every day to close down, so as to start preparing for the move. That had no difficulties, as we get so few visitors. But we could never quite make up our minds. It's your coming that has made us realize how thoroughly we'd abandoned any idea of going on with the business.

JAN: Am I to understand you definitely want to see me go?

MARTHA: As I said, we can't decide; I, especially, can't decide. Actually everything depends on me and I haven't made up my mind yet, one way or the other.

JAN: Please remember this; I don't want to be a burden on you and I shall behave exactly as you wish. However, I'd like to say that it will suit me if I can stay here for one or two days. I have some problems to thrash out before moving on, and I counted on finding here the peace and quietness I need.

MARTHA: I quite understand your desire, I assure you, and, if you like, I'll reconsider the matter. [*A short silence. She takes some steps hesitantly towards the door.*] Am I right in thinking you'll go back to the country from which you've come?

JAN: Yes – if necessary.

MARTHA: It's a pretty country, isn't it?

JAN [*looking out of the window*]: Yes, a very pretty country.

MARTHA: Is it true that there are long stretches of the coast where you never meet a soul?

JAN: Quite true. There's nothing to remind you that men exist. Sometimes at dawn you find the traces of birds' feet on the sand. Those are the only signs of life. And in the evenings . . .

MARTHA [*softly*]: Yes? What are the evenings like?

JAN: Marvellous, indescribable! Yes, it's a lovely country.

MARTHA [*in a tone she has not used before*]: I've thought of it, often and often. Travellers have told me things, and I've read what I could. And often, in the harsh, bleak spring we have here, I dream of the sea and the flowers over there. [*After a short silence, in a low, pensive voice*] And what I picture makes me blind to everything around me.

[*After gazing at her thoughtfully for some moments,* JAN *sits down facing her.*]

JAN: I can understand that. Spring over there grips you by the throat and flowers burst into bloom by thousands, above the white walls. If you roamed the hills that overlook my town for only an hour or so, you'd bring back in your clothes a sweet, honeyed smell of yellow roses.

[MARTHA, *too, sits down.*]

MARTHA: How wonderful that must be! What we call spring here is one rose and a couple of buds struggling to keep alive in the monastery garden. [*Scornfully*] And that's enough to stir the hearts of the men in this part of the world. Their hearts are as stingy as that rose-tree. A breath of richer air would wilt them; they have the springtime they deserve.

JAN: You're not quite fair; you have the autumn, too.

MARTHA: What's the autumn?

JAN: A second spring when every leaf's a flower. [*He looks at her keenly.*] Perhaps it's the same thing with some hearts; perhaps they'd blossom if you helped them with your patience.

MARTHA: I've no patience for this dreary Europe, where autumn has the face of spring and the spring smells of poverty. No, I prefer to picture those other lands over which summer breaks in flame, where the winter rains flood the cities, and where . . . things are what they are.

[*A short silence.* JAN *gazes at her with growing interest. She notices this and rises abruptly from the chair.*]

MARTHA: Why are you looking at me like that?

JAN: Sorry. But since we seem to have dropped our convention for the present, I don't see why I shouldn't tell you. It strikes me that, for the first time, you've been talking to me with – shall I say? – some human feeling.

MARTHA [*violently*]: Don't be too sure of that. And even if I have been, you've no cause for rejoicing. What you call human feeling is not the nicest part of me. What is human in me is what I desire, and to get what I desire, I'd stick at nothing, I'd sweep away every obstacle on my path.

JAN: I can understand that sort of violence. And I have no cause to let it frighten me, as I'm not an obstacle on your path, and I've no motive for opposing your desires.

MARTHA: Certainly you have no reason to oppose them. But it's equally true you have no reason for furthering them and, in some cases, that might bring things to a head.

JAN: Why be so sure I have no reason for furthering them?

MARTHA: Common sense tells me that; also my wish to keep you outside my plans.

JAN: Ah! That means, I take it, that we've returned to our conventions?

MARTHA: Yes, and we did wrong to depart from them – you can see that for yourself. Now it remains for me to thank you for having spoken of that country where you lived, and I must excuse myself for having, perhaps, wasted your time. [*She is on her way to the door.*] Still, let me tell you, the time was not wholly wasted. Our talk roused desires in me that were beginning to fall asleep. If you're really bent on staying here you've won your case without knowing it. When I entered this room I had almost decided to ask you to leave, but, as you see, you've played on my human feelings; now I hope you'll stay. And so my longing for the sea and sunshine will be the gainer by it.

[*He gazes at her without speaking for a moment.*]

JAN [*thoughtfully*]: You have a very strange way of talking. Still, if I may, and if your mother, too, has no objection, I'll stay on.

MARTHA: My mother's desires are weaker than mine; that's only natural. She doesn't think enough about the sea and those lonely beaches to make her realize you have got to stay. So she hasn't the same motives for wanting to keep you. But, at the same time, she hasn't any really strong motive for opposing me; and that will settle it.

JAN: So, if I've not misunderstood, one of you will let me stay for the sake of money, and the other through indifference.

MARTHA: What more can a traveller expect? But there's truth in what you said. [*She opens the door.*]

JAN: Well, I suppose I should be glad of that. Still perhaps you'll let me say that everything here strikes me as very strange; the people and their way of speaking. Really this is a queer house.

MARTHA: Perhaps that's only because you are behaving queerly in it. [*She goes out.*]

JAN [*looking towards the door*]: Maybe she's right. I wonder, though. [*Goes to the bed and sits down.*] Really the one wish that girl has given me is the wish to leave at once, to return to Maria and our happiness together. I've been behaving stupidly. What business have I to be here? . . . No, I have a reason, a good reason; I owe a duty to my mother and sister. I've neglected them too long. It's up to me to do something for them, to atone for my neglect. It's not enough in such cases to declare oneself, 'It's I.' One has to make oneself loved, as well. [*He rises.*] Yes, this is the room in which all will be decided. A wretchedly cold room, by the way. I can't recognize anything in it. Everything's been changed, and now it might be a bedroom in any one of those commercial hotels where men by themselves stay a night in passing. I've had experience of them, and I always used to think there was something they had to say – something like an answer or a message. Perhaps I shall get the answer here, tonight. [*He looks out of the window.*] Clouding up, I see. It's always like this in an hotel bedroom; the evenings are depressing for a lonely man. I can feel it again, that vague uneasiness I used to feel in the old days – here, in the hollow of my chest – like a raw place which the least movement irritates . . . And I know what it is. It's fear, fear of the eternal loneliness, fear that there is no answer. And who could there be to answer in an hotel bedroom?

[*He has moved to the bell; after some hesitation he puts his finger on the bell-push. For a while there is silence; then one hears approaching footsteps, a knock. The door opens. The old* MANSERVANT *is standing on the threshold. He neither moves nor speaks.*]

JAN: It's nothing. Sorry to have disturbed you. I only wanted to see if the bell was working and anyone would answer.

[*The old man stares at him, then closes the door. Receding footsteps.*]

JAN: The bell works, but *he* doesn't speak. That's no answer. [*He looks at the sky.*] The clouds are banking up still. A solid mass of darkness that will burst and fall upon the earth. What should I do? Which is right: Maria or my dreams?

[*Two knocks on the door.* MARTHA *enters with a tray.*]

JAN: What's this?

MARTHA: The tea you ordered.

JAN: But – I didn't order anything.

MARTHA: Oh? The old man must have heard wrong. He often understands badly. Still, as the tea is here, I suppose you'll have it? [*She puts the tray on the table.* JAN *makes a vague gesture.*] Don't trouble; it won't go down on the bill.

JAN: No, it isn't that. But I'm glad you brought me some tea. Most kind of you.

MARTHA: Please don't mention it. What we do is in our interests.

JAN: I can see you're determined not to leave me any illusions! But frankly I don't see where your interest comes in, in this case.

MARTHA: It does, I assure you. Sometimes a cup of tea's enough to keep our guests here. [*She goes out.*]

[JAN *picks up the cup, stares at it, puts it down again.*]

JAN: So the prodigal son's feast is continuing. First, a glass of beer – but in exchange for my money; then a cup of tea – because it encourages the visitor to stay on. But I'm to blame, too; I cannot strike the right note. When I'm confronted by that girl's almost brutal frankness, I search in vain for the words that would put things right between us. Of course, her part is simpler; it's easier to find words for a rebuff than those which reconcile. [*He picks up the cup, is silent for some moments, then continues in a low, tense voice.*] Oh God, give me the power to find my words aright, or else make me abandon this vain attempt, and return to Maria's love. And then give me the strength, once I have chosen, to abide by my choice. [*He raises the cup to his lips.*] The feast of the returning prodigal. The least I can do is to do it honour; and so I shall have played my part until I leave this place. [*He drinks. Loud knocking at the door.*] Who's there?

[*The door opens.* THE MOTHER *enters.*]

THE MOTHER: I'm sorry to disturb you, sir, but my daughter tells me she brought you some tea.

JAN: There it is.

THE MOTHER: Have you drunk it?

JAN: Yes. Why do you ask?

THE MOTHER: Excuse me, I've come to fetch the tray.

JAN [*smiling*]: I'm sorry this cup of tea is causing so much trouble.

THE MOTHER: It isn't quite that. But, as a matter of fact, that tea was not meant for you.

JAN: Ah, there's the explanation. It was brought without my having ordered it.

THE MOTHER [*wearily*]: Yes, that's it. It would have been better if . . . Anyhow that hasn't any great importance, whether you've drunk it or not.

JAN [*in a puzzled tone*]: I'm exceedingly sorry, I assure you, but your daughter insisted on leaving it, and I never imagined . . .

THE MOTHER: I'm sorry, too. But please don't excuse yourself. It was just a mistake. [*She puts the cup and saucer on the tray and moves towards the door.*]

JAN: Madame!

THE MOTHER: Yes?

JAN: I must apologize again. I've just come to a decision. I think I'll leave this evening, after dinner. Naturally I'll pay for the room, for the night. [*She gazes at him, in silence.*] I quite understand your looking surprised. But please don't imagine you are in any way responsible for my sudden change of plan. I have a great regard for you, a very great regard. But, to be candid, I don't feel at ease here, and I'd rather not stay the night.

THE MOTHER: That's quite all right, sir. Of course you can do exactly as you wish. Still, perhaps you may change your mind between now and dinner-time. Sometimes one yields to a passing impression, but, later on, things settle themselves and one gets used to new conditions.

JAN: I doubt it, madame. However, I would not like you to believe I am leaving because I'm dissatisfied with you.

On the contrary, I am very grateful to you for welcoming me as you have done. For, I must say, I seemed to notice you had a certain . . . friendliness towards me.

THE MOTHER: That was only natural, sir, and I'm sure you understand I had no personal reasons for showing any ill-will.

JAN [*with restrained emotion*]: That may be so – I hope so. But, if I told you that, it is because I want us to part on good terms. Later on, perhaps, I'll come back. In fact I'm sure I shall. And then things will certainly go better, and I've no doubt we shall find pleasure in meeting again. But just now I feel that I have made a mistake, I have no business to be here. In a word – though this may strike you as an odd way of putting it – I have a feeling that this house isn't for me.

THE MOTHER: I know what you mean, sir. But usually one feels that sort of thing immediately; you have been rather slow, it seems to me, to discover it.

JAN: I agree. But just now I'm rather at sea. I've come to Europe on some urgent business, and it's always a bit disconcerting, returning to a country after years and years of absence. I trust you understand what I mean.

THE MOTHER: Yes, I do understand, and I'd have liked things to turn out as you wished. But I think that, as far as we're concerned, there's nothing more we can do about it.

JAN: So it seems, I admit. Still, really, one never can be sure.

THE MOTHER: Anyhow, I think we have done everything needed to have you stay with us.

JAN: Indeed you have, and I've nothing to complain of. The truth is that you are the first people I have met since my return, so it's natural my first taste of the difficulties ahead should come when I'm with you. Obviously I alone am to blame for this; I haven't found my feet yet.

THE MOTHER: It's often like that in life; one makes a bad start, and nobody can do anything about it. In a way it's quite true that what has happened vexes me as well. But I tell myself that, after all, I've no reason to attach importance to it.

JAN: Well, it's something that you share my discomfort and that you try to understand me. I can hardly tell you how touched I am by your attitude, and how much I appreciate it. [*He stretches his hand towards her.*] Really I . . .

THE MOTHER: Oh, what you call my attitude's quite natural, really. It's our duty to make ourselves agreeable to our guests.

JAN [*in a disappointed tone*]: That's so. [*A short silence.*] So it comes to this: all I owe you is an apology and, if you think fit, some compensation. [*He draws his hand over his forehead. He seems exhausted and is speaking less easily.*] You may have made preparations, gone to some expense; so it's only fair . . .

THE MOTHER: The only preparations we've made are those we always make in such cases. And I can assure you that you owe us no compensation. It was not on our account that I was regretting your indecision, but on yours.

JAN [*leaning against the table*]: Oh, that doesn't matter. The great thing is that we understand each other and I shan't leave you with too bad an impression of myself. Personally I shall not forget this house – be sure of that – and I hope that when I return I'll be in a better mood to appreciate it. [*She goes to the door without speaking.*] Madame! [*She turns. He speaks with some difficulty, but ends more easily than he began.*] I'd like . . . Excuse me, but my journey's tired me. [*Sits on the bed.*] I'd like anyhow to thank you for the tea, and for the welcome you have given me. And I'd also like you to know that when I leave this house I shan't feel quite a stranger.

THE MOTHER: Really, sir, we have done very little for you. And please don't think I meant to be disagreeable about the tea; only it's a fact it wasn't meant for you. Being thanked for something due to a mistake is always embarrassing. [*She goes out.*]

[JAN *watches her, makes as if to move, but one can see he is feeling limp. Then, leaning his elbow on the pillow, he seems to abandon himself to his growing lethargy.*]

JAN: Yes, I must handle it quite simply, quite straightforwardly. Tomorrow I'll come here with Maria and I shall say 'It's I.' There's nothing to prevent my making them happy. Maria was right; I can see that now. [*He sighs, and leans back on the pillow.*] I don't like the feel of this evening; everything seems so far away. [*He stretches himself full-length on the bed, murmuring almost inaudibly*] Yes, or no?

[*After tossing about a little,* JAN *falls asleep. The room is in almost complete darkness. A long silence. The door opens. The two women enter, with a lamp.*]

MARTHA [*after holding the lamp above the sleeping man; in a whisper*]: All's well.

THE MOTHER [*in a low voice at first, but gradually raising it*]: No, Martha! I dislike having my hand forced like this. I'm being dragged into this act; you began it so that I'd have no chance of drawing back. I don't like your way of riding roughshod over my reluctance.

MARTHA: It is a way that simplifies everything. If you had given me any clear reason for your reluctance, I'd have been bound to consider it. But as you couldn't make up your mind, it was right for me to help you by taking the first step.

THE MOTHER: I know, of course, that it does not greatly matter; this man or some other, today or some later day, tonight or tomorrow – it had to come to that. None the less, I don't feel pleased about it.

MARTHA: Come, mother! Think of tomorrow, instead, and let's get busy. Our freedom will begin when this night ends. [*She unbuttons Jan's coat, extracts his wallet, and counts the notes.*]

THE MOTHER: How soundly he's sleeping!

MARTHA: He's sleeping as they all slept . . . Now let's start.

THE MOTHER: Wait a little, please. Isn't it strange how helpless and defenceless men look when they're asleep?

MARTHA: It's a rest they take before becoming again the savage brutes or silly apes they all are.

THE MOTHER [*meditatively*]: No, men aren't quite so remarkable as you seem to think, and really they don't change when they're asleep. It's we who look at them with different eyes, and the sudden nakedness of their faces, without any glow of passion or frown of discontent, takes us aback. But of course you, Martha, don't know what I mean.

MARTHA: No, mother, I don't. But I do know that we are wasting time.

THE MOTHER [*with a sort of weary irony*]: Oh, there's no such hurry. On the contrary, this is the moment we can relax, now that the main thing's done. It's not the act itself that counts, but the embarking on it. Once a start is made, one's peace of mind returns. Why work yourself up like this? Is it really worth while?

MARTHA: Nothing's worth while, the moment one talks about it. It's better to get on with the work in hand and ask no questions of oneself.

THE MOTHER [*calmly*]: Let's sit down, Martha.

MARTHA: Here? Beside him?

THE MOTHER: Certainly. Why not? He has entered on a sleep that will take him far, and it's not likely he will wake up and inquire what we're doing here. As for the rest of the world – it stops short at that closed door. Why shouldn't we enjoy this little breathing space in peace?

MARTHA: You're joking, and it's my turn to tell you I don't appreciate your way of talking.

THE MOTHER: You're wrong. I don't feel in the least like joking. I'm merely showing calmness while you are letting your nerves run wild. No, Martha, sit down [*she gives a curious laugh*] and look at that man who's even more innocent in sleep than in his talk. He, anyhow, is through with the world. From now on, everything will be easy for him. He will pass from a dreamful sleep into dreamless sleep. And what for others is a cruel wrench will be for him no more than a protracted rest.

MARTHA: Innocence has the sleep that innocence deserves. And this man, anyhow, I had no reason for hating. So I'm glad he is being spared any pain. But I've no reason, either, for looking at him, and I think it a bad idea of yours, staring like that at a man whom presently you'll have to carry.

THE MOTHER [*shaking her head; in a low voice*]: When the hour comes we shall carry him. But we still have time in hand and perhaps it won't be such a bad idea – for him at any rate – if we look at him attentively. For it's not too late yet; sleep isn't death. Yes, Martha, look at him. He is living through a moment when he has no say in his fate; when his hopes of life are made over to indifferent hands. Let these hands stay as they are, folded in my lap, until the dawn and, without his knowing anything, he'll have entered on a new lease of life. But if they move towards him and form a hard ring round his ankles, he will lie in an unremembered grave for ever.

MARTHA [*rising brusquely*]: Mother, you're forgetting that all nights end, and we have much to do. First, we must look through the papers in his pockets and carry him downstairs. Then we'll have to put out all the lights and keep watch in the doorway as long as needs be.

THE MOTHER: Yes, there is much for us to do, and that is where we are in a different case from his; he, at least, is free now of the burden of his life. He has done with the anxiety of making decisions, with thoughts of work that must be done, with strain and stress. A cross is lifted from his shoulders; the cross of that inner life which allows of no repose, no weakness, no relaxing. At this moment he exacts nothing of himself and, old and tired as I am, I almost think that there lies happiness.

MARTHA: We've no time for wondering where happiness lies. When I have kept watch as long as needs be, there will still be much to do. We shall have to go down to the river and make sure some drunk man isn't sleeping on the bank. Then we'll have to carry him down there as quickly as we can – and you know the effort that means. We shall have to do it in several stages and, once we are on the bank, swing him out as far as possible into mid stream. And let me remind you again that nights don't last for ever.

THE MOTHER: Yes, all that lies before us, and the mere thought of it makes me tired, with a tiredness that has lasted so long that my old blood can't cope with it. And, meanwhile, this man has no suspicion; he is enjoying his repose. If we let him wake he'll have to start life again and, from what I've seen of him, I know he is much like other men and cannot live in peace. Perhaps that is why we must take him there and make him over to the mercy of the dark water. [*She sighs.*] But it's a sad thing so much effort should be needed to rid a man of his follies and put him in the way of peace.

MARTHA: I can only think, mother, that your wits are wandering. I repeat, we have much to do. Once he's thrown in, we shall have to efface the marks on the river bank, blur our footsteps on the path, destroy his clothes and baggage – make him vanish from the face of the earth, in fact. Time's passing and soon it will be too late to carry all this out with the composure that it needs. Really I cannot understand what has come over you, to be sitting at that man's bedside and staring at him, though you can hardly see him, and persisting in this absurd, useless talk.

THE MOTHER: Tell me, Martha. Did you know that he meant to leave this evening?

MARTHA: No, I didn't. But if I'd known, it wouldn't have changed anything, once I had made up my mind.

THE MOTHER: He told me that just now, and I didn't know how to answer him.

MARTHA: Ah! So you had a talk with him?

THE MOTHER: Yes, when you said you'd brought his tea, I came here. I'd have stopped him from drinking it, if I had been in time. As it was, once I knew the beginning had been made, I felt we'd better let things take their course; really it hadn't much importance.

MARTHA: If you still feel like that, there's no reason for dawdling here. So please get up from that chair and help me finish off this business – which is getting on my nerves.

THE MOTHER [*rising*]: Yes, I suppose I'll end by helping you. Only you might allow a few minutes more to an old woman whose blood doesn't flow as fast as yours. You've been on the rush ever since this morning, and you expect me to keep pace with you! Even that man there couldn't manage it; before he had framed the thought of leaving, he'd drunk the tea you gave him.

MARTHA: If you must know, it was he who made up my mind for me. You talked me into sharing your reluctance. But then he started telling me about those countries where I've always longed to go, and by working on my feelings hardened my heart against him. Thus innocence is rewarded.

THE MOTHER: And yet he'd come to understand. He said he felt that this house was not his home.

MARTHA [*violently and impatiently*]: Of course it is not his home. For that matter it is nobody's home. No one will ever find warmth or comfort or contentment in this house. Had he realized that sooner, he'd have been spared, and spared us, too. He would have spared our having to teach him that this room is made for sleeping in, and this world for dying in. Come, mother, and for the sake of the God you sometimes call on, let's have done with it.

[THE MOTHER *takes a step towards the bed.*]

THE MOTHER: Very well, Martha, we'll begin. But I have a feeling that tomorrow's dawn will never come.

CURTAIN

ACT THREE

The inn-parlour. THE MOTHER, MARTHA, *and the* MANSERVANT *are on the stage. The old man is sweeping and tidying up the room;* MARTHA, *standing behind the bar counter, drawing back her hair.* THE MOTHER *is walking towards the door.*

MARTHA: Well, you see that dawn has come and we've got through the night without mishap.

THE MOTHER: Yes. And tomorrow I'll be thinking it's a good thing to have done with it. But, just now, all I feel is that I'm dead tired and my heart's dried up within me. Ah, it was a hard night indeed!

MARTHA: But this morning is the first for years when I breathe freely. Never did a killing cost me less. I almost seem to hear the waves already, and I feel like crying out for joy.

THE MOTHER: So much the better, Martha. So much the better. As for me, I feel so old this morning that I can't share anything with you. But perhaps tomorrow I'll be in a better way.

MARTHA: Yes, and everything will, I hope, be better. But do please stop complaining and give me a chance of relishing my new-found happiness. I'm like a young girl again this morning; I feel my blood flowing warm, and I want to run about and sing! . . . Oh, mother, may I ask you something . . . [*Pauses.*]

THE MOTHER: What's come over you, Martha? You're like a different person.

MARTHA: Mother . . . [*Hesitates; then in a rush*] Tell me, am I still pretty?

THE MOTHER: Yes, I think you're looking really pretty this morning. Some acts seem to have a good effect on you.

MARTHA: Oh, no! Those acts you mean lie on me so lightly. But this morning I feel as if I'd been born again, to a new life; at last I'm going to a country where I shall be happy.

THE MOTHER: No doubt, no doubt. And, once I've got over my tiredness, I, too, shall breathe freely. Even now, it makes up for all those sleepless nights of ours, to know they'll have brought you happiness. But this morning I must rest; all I'm conscious of is that the night has been a hard one.

MARTHA: What does last night matter? Today is a great day. [*To the servant*] Keep your eyes open when you're sweeping; we dropped some of his papers on the way out and I couldn't stop to pick them up. They're on the floor somewhere. [THE MOTHER *leaves the room. Sweeping under a table, the old man comes on Jan's passport, opens it, runs his eyes over it, and hands it, open, to Martha.*] I don't need to see it. Put it with the other things; we'll burn them all together. [*The old man goes on holding the passport to Martha. She takes it.*] What is it? [*The old man goes out.* MARTHA *reads the passport slowly, without showing any emotion; then calls in a voice that sounds completely calm*] Mother!

THE MOTHER [*from the next room*]: What do you want now?

MARTHA: Come here.

[THE MOTHER *returns.* MARTHA *gives her the passport.*]

MARTHA: Read!

THE MOTHER: You know quite well my eyes are tired.

MARTHA: Read!

[THE MOTHER *takes the passport, sits at the table, spreads it open, and reads. For a long while she stares at the page in front of her.*]

THE MOTHER [*in a toneless voice*]: Yes, I always knew it would turn out like this one day – and that would be the end. The end of all!

MARTHA [*coming from behind the bar counter, and standing in front of it*]: Mother!

THE MOTHER: No, Martha, let me have my way; I've lived quite long enough. I have lived many years more than my son. That isn't as it should be. Now I can go and join him at the bottom of the river, where already the weeds have covered up his face.

MARTHA: Mother! Surely you won't leave me alone?

THE MOTHER: You have been a great help to me, Martha, and I am sorry to leave you. If such words have any meaning left for us, I can honestly say you were a good daughter, in your fashion. You have always shown me the respect you owed me. But now I am very weary; my old heart, which seemed indifferent to everything, has learnt again today what grief means, and I'm not young enough to come to terms with it. In any case, when a mother is no longer capable of recognizing her own son, it's clear her role on earth is ended.

MARTHA: No. Not if her daughter's happiness remains to be ensured. And, no less than my heart, my hopes are shattered when I hear you speaking in this new, amazing way – you who had taught me to respect nothing.

THE MOTHER [*in the same listless tone*]: It only proves that in a world where everything can be denied, there are forces undeniable; and on this earth where nothing's sure we have our certainties. [*Bitterly*] And a mother's love for her son is now my certainty.

MARTHA: So you are not sure that a mother can love her daughter?

THE MOTHER: It's not now I'd want to wound you, Martha, but love for a daughter can never be the same thing. It strikes less deep. And how could I now live without my son's love?

MARTHA: A wonderful love – that forgot you utterly for twenty years!

THE MOTHER: Yes, it was a wonderful love that outlasted twenty years of silence and brought back to his home a son who seemed forgetful as he was forgotten. Say what you will, that love is wonderful enough for me – since I can't live without it. [*She rises from her chair.*]

MARTHA: It's not possible you can talk like that, without any thought for your daughter, without the least stirring of revolt!

THE MOTHER: Hard as it is on you, it *is* possible. I have no thought for anything; still less any feeling of revolt. No doubt this is my punishment, and for all murderers a time comes when, like me, they are dried up within, sterile, with nothing left to live for. That's why society gets rid of them; they're good for nothing.

MARTHA: I can't bear to hear you talking like that, about crime and punishment; it's . . . despicable!

THE MOTHER: I'm not troubling to pick my words; I've ceased to have any preference. But it's true that by one act I have ruined everything. I have lost my freedom and my hell has begun.

MARTHA [*going up to her mother; fiercely*]: You never spoke like that before. During all these years you've stood beside me, and your hands never flinched from gripping the legs of those who were to die. A lot you thought of hell or freedom in those days! It never occurred to you that you had no right to live, and you went on – doing as you did. What change can your son have brought to that?

THE MOTHER: I went on with it; that's true. But what I lived through then, I lived through by dint of habit, which is not so very different from death. An experience of grief was enough to change all that, and my son's coming has brought that change. [MARTHA *makes a gesture and seems about to speak.*] Oh I know, Martha, that doesn't make sense. What has a criminal to do with grief? But I'd have you notice that my grief is not the wild grief that mothers feel; I haven't raised my voice as yet. It's no more than the pain of feeling love rekindle in my heart; and yet it's too much for me. I know that this pain, too, doesn't make sense. [*In a changed tone*] But then this world we live in doesn't make sense, and I have a right to judge it, since I've tested all it has to offer, from creation to destruction. [*She walks resolutely towards the door.*]

[MARTHA *slips in front of her and bars the way.*]

MARTHA: No, mother, you shall not leave me. Don't forget that it was I who stayed beside you, and *he* went away. For a whole lifetime I have been with you, and he left you in silence. That must come into the reckoning. That must be paid for. And it's your duty to come back to me.

THE MOTHER [*gently*]: That's true enough, Martha. But he, my son, was killed by me.

[MARTHA *has half-turned away and seems to be gazing at the door.*]

MARTHA [*after a short silence, with rising emotion*]: All that life can give a man was given him. He left this country. He came to know far horizons, the sea, free beings. But I stayed here, eating my heart out in the shadows, small and insignificant, buried alive in a gloomy valley in the heart of Europe. Buried alive! No one has ever kissed my mouth and no one, not even you, has seen me naked. Mother, I swear to you, that *must* be paid for. And now, when at last I am to get what's due to me, you cannot, *must* not desert me on the vain pretext that a man is dead. Do try to understand that for a man who has lived his life death is a little thing. We can forget my brother and your son. What has happened to him has no importance; he had nothing more to get from life. But for me it's different, and you are spoiling me of everything, cheating me of the pleasures he enjoyed. Why must that man deprive me of my mother's love as well and drag you down with him into the icy darkness of the river? [*They gaze silently at each other;* MARTHA *lowers her eyes. She speaks now in a very low voice.*] I ask so little, so very little of life. Mother, there are words I never could bring myself to use, but – don't you think it would be soothing if we started our life again just as it used to be, you and I together?

THE MOTHER: Did you recognize him?

MARTHA: No, I didn't. I had not the slightest recollection of what he looked like, and everything happened as it was bound to happen. You said it yourself; this world doesn't make sense. But you weren't altogether wrong in asking me that question. For I know now that if I'd recognized him, it would have made no difference.

THE MOTHER: I prefer to think that isn't true. No soul is wholly criminal, and the wickedest murderers have moments when they lay down their arms.

MARTHA: I have such moments, too. But I would not have lowered my head to a brother whom I did not know and who meant nothing to me.

THE MOTHER: To whom then would you lower your head?

[MARTHA *lowers her head.*]

MARTHA: To you.

[*A short silence.*]

THE MOTHER [*quietly*]: Too late, Martha. I can do nothing more for you. [*Half-averting her eyes*] Oh, why did he keep silence? Silence is fatal. But speaking is as dangerous; the little he said hurried it on. [*Turns towards her daughter.*] Are you crying, Martha? No, you wouldn't know how to cry. Can you remember the time when I used to kiss you?

MARTHA: No, mother.

THE MOTHER: I understand. It was so long ago, and I forgot so soon to hold out my arms to you. But I never ceased loving you. [*She gently thrusts aside Martha, who gradually makes way for her.*] I know it now; now that your brother's coming has brought to life again that intolerable love which I now must kill – together with myself.

[*The doorway is free for her to pass.*]

MARTHA [*burying her face in her hands*]: But what, oh what can mean more to you than your daughter's grief?

THE MOTHER: Weariness, perhaps . . . and my longing for rest. [*She goes out.*]

[MARTHA *makes no effort to detain her. Once her mother has left she runs to the door, slams it to, and presses herself against it. She breaks into loud, fierce cries.*]

MARTHA: No, no! What concern of mine was it to look after my brother? None whatever! And yet now I'm an outcast in my own home, there is no place for me to lay my head, my own mother will have none of me. No, it wasn't my duty to look after him – oh the unfairness of it all, the injustice done to innocence! For he – he now has what he wanted, while I am left lonely, far from the sea I longed for. Oh, how I hate him! All my life was spent waiting for this great wave that was to lift me up and sweep me far away, and now I know it will never come again. I am doomed to stay here with all those other countries, other nations, on my left hand and my right, before me and behind; all those plains and mountains that are barriers to the salt winds blowing from the sea, and the rumour of whose voices drowns its low, unceasing summons. [*In a lower tone*] There are places to which, far as they may be from the sea, the evening wind brings sometimes a smell of seaweed. It tells of moist sea beaches, loud with the cries of seagulls, or of golden sands bathed in a sunset glow that has no limit. But the sea winds fail long before they reach this place. Never, never shall I have what's due to me. I may press my ear to the earth but I shall not hear the crash of icy breakers, or the measured breathing of a happy sea. I am too far from all I love, and my exile is beyond remedy. I hate him, yes, I hate him for having got what he wanted! My only home is in this gloomy, shut-in country where the sky has no horizons; for my hunger I have nothing but the sour Moravian sloes, for my thirst only the blood that I have shed. That is the price one must pay for a mother's love!

There is no love for me, so let her die. Let every door be shut against me; all I wish is to be left in peace with my anger, my very rightful anger. For I have no intention of rolling my eyes heavenwards or pleading for forgiveness before I die. In that southern land, guarded by the sea, to which one can escape, where one can breathe freely, press one's body to another's body, roll in the waves – to that sea-guarded land the gods have no access. But here one's gaze is cramped on every side, everything is planned to make one look up in humble supplication. I hate this narrow world in which we are reduced to gazing up at God.

But I have not been given my rights and I am smarting from the injustice done me; I will not bend my knee. I have been cheated of my place on earth, cast away by my mother, left alone with my crimes, and I shall leave this world without being reconciled. [*A knock at the door.*] Who's there?

MARIA: A traveller.

MARTHA: We're not taking any guests now.

MARIA: But my husband's here. I have come to see him. [*Enters.*]

MARTHA [*staring at her*]: Your husband. Who's that?

MARIA: He came here yesterday evening and he promised

to call for me this morning. I can't understand why he didn't come.

MARTHA: He said his wife was abroad.

MARIA: He had special reasons for that. But we'd arranged to meet this morning.

MARTHA [*who has kept her eyes fixed on Maria*]: That may be difficult. Your husband's gone.

MARIA: Gone? I don't follow. Didn't he book a room here?

MARTHA: Yes, but he left it during the night.

MARIA: Really I can't believe that. I know his reasons for wanting to stay in this house. But the way you speak alarms me. Please tell me frankly whatever you have to tell.

MARTHA: I have nothing to tell you, except that your husband is no longer here.

MARIA: I simply cannot understand; he would not have gone away without me. Did he say that he was going for good, or that he'd come back?

MARTHA: He has left us for good.

MARIA: Please listen. I can't bear to be kept in suspense any longer. Since yesterday I've been waiting, waiting, in this strange land, and now my anxiety has brought me to this house. I will not go away before I have seen my husband or been told where I can find him.

MARTHA: Your husband's whereabouts is your concern, not mine.

MARIA: You are wrong. You, too, are concerned in this, and closely. I don't know if my husband will approve of my telling you this, but I'm sick and tired of this futile game of make-believe. The man who came here yesterday is the brother you'd heard nothing of for years and years.

MARTHA: That's no news to me.

MARIA [*violently*]: Then – what can have happened? If everything has been cleared up, how is it Jan's not here?

Did you not welcome him home, you and your mother, and weren't you full of joy at his return?

MARTHA: My brother is no longer here – because he is dead.

[MARIA *gives a start and stares at Martha for some moments without speaking. Then she takes a step towards her, smiling.*]

MARIA: Ah, you're joking, of course. Jan's often told me that when you were little you loved mystifying people. You and I are almost sisters and –

MARTHA: Don't touch me. Stay where you are. There is nothing in common between us. [*Pauses.*] I can assure you I'm not joking; your husband died last night. So there's no reason for you to stay here any longer.

MARIA: But you're mad, stark staring mad! People don't die like that – when one's arranged to meet them, from one moment to the other, all of a sudden. I can't believe you. Let me see him and then I may believe what I can't even imagine.

MARTHA: That's impossible. He's at the bottom of the river. [MARIA *stretches her hand towards her.*] Don't touch me! Stay there. I repeat; he is at the bottom of the river. My mother and I carried him to the river last night, after putting him to sleep. He didn't suffer, but he is dead sure enough, and it was we, his mother and I, who killed him.

MARIA [*shrinking away*]: It must be I who am mad. I'm hearing words that have never before been said on this earth. I knew that no good would come to me here, but this is sheer craziness and I will not share in it. At the very moment when your words strike death into my heart, it seems to me that you are talking of some other man, not of the man who shared my nights, and all this is a tale of long ago, in which my love never had a part.

MARTHA: It's not for me to convince you; only to tell you the truth. A truth which you will have to recognize before long.

MARIA [*in a sort of reverie*]: But why, *why* did you do it?

MARTHA: What right have you to question me?

MARIA [*passionately*]: What right? . . . My love for him.

MARTHA: What does that word mean?

MARIA: It means – it means all that at this moment is tearing, gnawing at my heart; it means this rush of frenzy that makes my fingers itch for murder. It means all my past joys, and this wild, sudden grief you have brought me. Yes, you crazy woman, if it wasn't that I've steeled my heart against believing, you'd learn the meaning of that word, when you felt my nails scoring your cheeks.

MARTHA: Again, you are using language I cannot understand. Words like love and joy and grief are meaningless to me.

MARIA [*making a great effort to speak calmly*]: Listen, Martha – that's your name, isn't it? Let's stop this game, if game it is, of cross-purposes. Let's have done with useless words. Tell me quite clearly what I want to know quite clearly, before I let myself break down.

MARTHA: Surely I made it clear enough. We did to your husband last night what we had done to other travellers, before; we killed him and took his money.

MARIA: So his mother and sister were criminals?

MARTHA: Yes. But that's their business, and no one else's.

MARIA [*still controlling herself with an effort*]: Had you learnt he was your brother when you did it?

MARTHA: If you *must* know, there was a misunderstanding. And if you have any experience at all of the world, that won't surprise you.

MARIA [*going towards the table, her hands clenched on her breast; in a low, sad voice*]: Oh, my God, I knew it! I knew this play-acting was bound to end in tragedy and we'd be punished, he and I, for having lent ourselves to it. I felt danger in the very air one breathes in this country. [*She stops in front of the table and goes on speaking, without looking at Martha.*] He wanted to make his homecoming a surprise, to get you to recognize him and to bring you happiness. Only at first he couldn't find the words that were needed. And then, while he was groping for the words, he was killed. [*Weeping*] And you, like two madwomen, blind to the marvellous son who had returned to you – for marvellous he was, and you will never know the greatheartedness, the noble soul, of the man you killed last night. . . . He might have been your pride, as he was mine. But, no, you were his enemy – oh, the pity of it! – for else how could you bring yourself to speak so calmly of what should make you rush into the street, screaming out your heart, like a wounded animal?

MARTHA: You have no right to sit in judgement without knowing all. By now my mother's lying with her son, pressed to the sluice-gate, and the current is beginning to gnaw their faces, and buffeting them against the rotting piles. Soon their bodies will be drawn up and buried together in the same earth. But I cannot see what there is even in this to set me screaming with pain. I have a very different idea of the human heart, and, to be frank, your tears revolt me.

MARIA [*swinging round on her fiercely*]: My tears are for the joys I've lost for ever; for a life's happiness stolen from me. And this is better for you than the tearless grief I shall have presently, which could kill you without the flutter of an eyelid.

MARTHA: Do not imagine talk like that affects me; really it would make little difference. For I, too, have seen and heard enough; I, too, have resolved to die. But I shall not join them; why, indeed, would I want their company? I shall leave them to their new-found love, to their dark embraces. Neither you nor I have any part in these; all that is ended and they are unfaithful to us – for ever. Luckily I have my bedroom and the roof-tree's strong.

MARIA: What does it matter to me that you die or the whole world falls in ruins, if through you I have lost the man I love, and henceforth I am doomed to live in a dark night of loneliness, where every memory is torture?

[MARTHA *comes behind her and speaks over her head.*]

MARTHA: Don't let's exaggerate. You have lost your husband and I have lost my mother. We are quits. But you have only lost him once, after enjoying his love for years and without his having cast you off. My lot is worse. First my mother cast me off, and now she is dead. I have lost her twice.

MARIA: Yes, perhaps I might be tempted to pity you and share my grief with you, did I not know what was awaiting him, alone in his room, last night, when you were plotting his death.

MARTHA [*her voice has a sudden accent of despair*]: I'm quits with your husband, too, for I have suffered as he suffered. Like him, I thought I had made sure my home for always; I thought that crime had forged a bond between me and my mother that nothing could ever break. And on whom in all the world should I rely, if not on the woman who had killed beside me? I was mistaken. Crime, too, means solitude, even if a thousand people join together to commit it. And it is fitting that I should die alone, after having lived and killed alone.

[MARIA *turns towards her, tears streaming down her cheeks.* MARTHA *moves back; her voice grows hard again.*]

MARTHA: Stop! I told you not to touch me. At the mere thought that a human hand could lay its warmth on me before I die; at the mere thought that anything at all resembling the foul love of men is dogging me still, I feel the blood pulsing in my temples in a fury of disgust.

[MARIA *has risen to her feet. The two women now are face to face, standing very near each other.*]

MARIA: Have no fear. I shall do nothing to prevent your dying as you wish. For with this hideous pain that grips my body like a vice, I feel a sort of blindness falling on my eyes and everything around me is growing dim. Neither you nor your mother will ever be more to me than vague, fleeting faces that came and went in the course of a tragedy which can never end. For you, Martha, I have no hatred and no pity. I have lost the power of loving or hating anybody. [*Suddenly she buries her face in her hands.*] But then – I have hardly had time to suffer or to rebel. My calamity was . . . too big for me.

MARTHA [*who has taken some steps towards the door, comes back towards Maria*]: But still not big enough; it has left you eyes to weep with. And I see that something remains for me to do before leaving you for ever. I have yet to drive you to despair.

MARIA [*gazing at her, horror-stricken*]: Oh, please leave me alone! Go away, and let me be!

MARTHA: Yes, I am going, and it will be a relief for me, as well. Your love and your tears are odious to me. But before I go to die, I must rid you of the illusion that you are right, that love isn't futile, and that what has happened was an accident. On the contrary, it's now that we are in the normal order of things, and I must convince you of it.

MARIA: What do you mean by that?

MARTHA: That in the normal order of things no one is ever recognized.

MARIA [*distractedly*]: Oh, what do I care? I only know that my heart is torn to shreds, and nothing, nothing matters to it except the man you killed.

MARTHA [*savagely*]: Be silent! I will not have you speak of that man; I loathe him. And he is nothing to you now. He has gone down into the bitter house of eternal exile. The fool! Well, he has got what he wanted; he is with the woman he crossed the sea to find. So all of us are served now, as we should be, in the order of things. But fix this in your mind; neither for him nor for us, neither in life nor in death, is there any peace or homeland. [*With a scornful laugh*] For you'll agree one can hardly call it a home, that place of clotted darkness underground, to which we go from here, to feed blind animals.

MARIA [*weeping*]: I can't, oh no, I can't bear to hear you talk like that. And I know he, too, wouldn't have borne it. It was to find another homeland that he crossed the sea.

MARTHA [*who has walked to the door, swings round on her*]: His folly has received its wages. And soon you will receive yours. [*Laughing as before*] We're cheated, I tell you. Cheated! What do they serve, those blind impulses that surge up in us, the yearnings that rack our souls? Why cry out for the sea, or for love? What futility! Your husband knows now what the answer is: that charnel house where in the end we shall lie huddled together, side by side. [*Vindictively*] A time will come when you, too, know it, and then, could you remember anything, you would recall as a delightful memory this day which seems to you the beginning of the cruellest of exiles. Try to realize that no grief of yours can ever equal the injustice done to man.

And now – before I go, let me give a word of advice; I owe it to you, since I killed your husband. Pray your God to harden you to stone. It's the happiness He has assigned Himself, and the one true happiness. Do as He does, be deaf to all appeals, and turn your heart to stone while there still is time. But if you feel you lack the courage to enter into this hard, blind peace – then come and join us in our common house. Good-bye, my sister. As you see, it's all quite simple. You have a choice between the mindless happiness of stones and the slimy bed in which we are awaiting you. [*She goes out.*]

[MARIA, *who has been listening in horrified amazement, sways, stretching out her arms in front of her.*]

MARIA [*her voice rising to a scream*]: Oh God, I cannot live in this desert! It is on You that I must call, and I shall find the words to say. [*She sinks on her knees.*] I place myself in your hands. Have pity, turn towards me. Hear me and raise me from the dust, oh Heavenly Father! Have pity on those who love each other and are parted.

[*The door opens. The old* MANSERVANT *is standing on the threshold.*]

THE OLD MANSERVANT [*in a clear, firm tone*]: What's all this noise? Did you call me?

MARIA [*gazing at him*]: Oh! . . . I don't know. But help me, help me, for I need help. Be kind and say that you will help me.

THE OLD MANSERVANT [*in the same tone*]: No.

CURTAIN

Some more Penguin Books are described overleaf

Also by Albert Camus

THE OUTSIDER

Meursault is a young man who lives in the usual manner of a French-Algerian, middle-class bachelor ... but he has a glaring fault in the eyes of society – he seems to lack the basic emotions and reactions (including hypocrisy) that are required of him. He observes the facts of life, death, and sex from the outside.

THE PLAGUE

The Times described it as a 'carefully wrought metaphysical novel the machinery of which can be compared to a Sophoclean tragedy. The plague in question afflicted Oran in the 1940s; and on one plane the book is a straightforward narrative. Into it, however, can be read all Camus's native anxieties, centred on the idea of plague as a symbol.'

THE FALL

Jean-Baptiste Clamence appeared to himself and to others the epitome of good citizenship and decent behaviour. Suddenly he sees through the deep-seated hypocrisy of his existence to the condescension which motivates his every action. He turns to debauchery, and finally settles in Amsterdam where, a self-styled 'judge penitent', he describes his fall to a chance acquaintance.

EXILE AND THE KINGDOM

These six short stories show the same qualities that won a Nobel Prize for Literature for the late Albert Camus. Four of them are set in Algeria on the fringes of the desert – an environment which has often been associated with deep mystical and emotional experience.

THE REBEL

It is not only the best book Camus has written, but one of the vital works of our time, compassionate and disillusioned, intelligent but instructed by deeply felt experience.

Camus himself described this work as 'an attempt to understand the time I live in'.

Jean-Paul Sartre

ALTONA
MEN WITHOUT SHADOWS
THE FLIES

Born in Paris in 1905, Jean-Paul Sartre studied philosophy and took up teaching. After service in the Resistance he became a writer and edits *Les Temps Modernes.* His philosophical books – notably *L'Être et le néant* (1943) – have caused him to be regarded as the founder of existentialism. His novels, such as *The Age of Reason* (now in Penguins), tend to stress the meaningless aspect of modern life.

His plays, on the other hand, deal more with human freedom. *The Flies* (1942) presents Sartre's interpretation of the Greek legend of Orestes. *Men Without Shadows* (1946) is a brutal study of the effects of torture on captured members of the Maquis. *Altona* (1959, previously published as *Loser Wins*) comments on the acquisitive aspects of capitalism as seen in a family of rich German industrialists.

Noson boring i mewn

pen dafad

Noson boring i mewn

Alun Jones a Nia Royles (gol.)

Hoffai'r Lolfa ddiolch i:
Ddisgyblion Blwyddyn 9, Ysgol Brynrefail
Karina Perry, Ysgol Caeraenion,
Dafydd Roberts, Ysgol Dyffryn Ogwen,
Steven Mason, Ysgol Uwchradd Llanfair ym Muallt
ac Elizabeth John, Ysgol y Preseli

Argraffiad cyntaf: 2003

Golygyddion Pen Dafad: Alun Jones a Nia Royles
Cynllun a llun clawr: Ceri Jones

Comisiynwyd y gyfrol gyda chymorth ariannol Awdurdod Cymwysterau, Cwricwlwm ac Asesu Cymru

ISBN: 0 86243 701 6

Cyhoeddwyd ac argraffwyd yng Nghymru gan:
Y Lolfa Cyf., Talybont, Ceredigion SY24 5AP
e-bost ylolfa@ylolfa.com
gwefan www.ylolfa.com
ffôn +44 (0)1970 832 304
ffacs 832 782
isdn 832 813

Cynnwys

Noson boring i mewn
gan Owain Meredith

Roedd hi'n noson oer a gwyntog wrth i Rhys Jones gerdded adre. Tŷ ffarm oedd Maesgwyn ar waelod chwarter milltir o ffordd breifat garegog a thyllog.

Roedd Rhys wedi cerdded y ffordd hon ers pan oedd o'n blentyn a chan ei fod yn gwybod yn union lle i gamu, hyd yn oed yn y tywyllwch, roedd cerdded adre'n gyfle perffaith i feddwl am waith ysgol neu be oedd wedi digwydd yn yr ysgol, a phwy roedd o'n ei ffansïo. Pob math o bethau.

Ond, heno, roedd hi'n noson wyllt a stormus, yn adlewyrchu'n berffaith gyflwr meddwl Rhys. Roedd ei fennydd yn llawn bustl a pharddu. Rhedai finegr casineb drwy wythiennau ei ben ac roedd sŵn rhyfel yng nghuriad ei galon. Na, doedd Rhys ddim wedi cael diwrnod da iawn o gwbwl.

Y peth cynta a aeth o'i le oedd ei fod wedi chwerthin yn y gwasanaeth ar ôl i Mathew Creed sibrwd y gair 'rhech' yn ei glust dde. Nid y gair oedd yn ddoniol, mewn gwirionedd, ond roedd wyneb mwnci, eiddgar Mathew yn edrych mor chwerthinllyd. I ddechrau, roedd Rhys wedi troi ei gefn a syllu ar y llwyfan gan ddangos diddordeb anarferol yn yr hyn roedd y prifathro yn ei ddweud. Ond roedd o'n gwybod bod Mathew yn dal i edrych yn wirion arno fo. Ceisiodd fygu'r chwerthin i ddechrau drwy wneud stumiau rhyfedd â'i wyneb. Yna ceisiodd feddwl am bethau trist fel marwolaeth Tomi'r gath dan olwynion y tractor yr haf cynt. Ond, ar ôl ychydig, dechreuodd ysgwyd a chrio chwerthin.

Wedyn, cafodd hergwd o'r tu ôl gan Mr Durman, yr athro Addysg Grefyddol, a'i hel i sefyll o flaen yr ysgol i gyd. Doedd ganddo ddim syniad pam roedd yr hyn ddywedodd Mathew yn ddoniol o gwbwl. Roedd pum munud o sefyll fel llo o flaen yr ysgol wedi teimlo fel ugain mlynedd o artaith. Dyna oedd Mathew yn licio'i neud – chwarae'r ffŵl a chreu trafferth. Pawb arall fyddai'n ei chael hi bob tro.

Fel yr wythnos diwethaf, pan oedd Mathew wedi sicrhau bod Helen Sharpe a'i ffrindia sgrechlyd yn y stafell newid pan oedd Rhys yn cael cawod ar ôl chwarae pump bob ochr. Roedd Helen a Mathew yn lladd eu hunain yn chwerthin wrth i Rhys gerddded allan o'r gawod yn hollol borcyn a Mathew, y bastad bach, yn gwybod yn iawn fod Rhys yn ffansïo Helen. Ond, dyna fo, Mathew oedd ei ffrind gorau.

Wrth i Rhys agosáu at Maesgwyn, sylwodd fod rhywbeth o'i le. Wrth iddo groesi'r grid gwartheg ar ben y ffordd a chamu ar y buarth, sylwodd nad oedd golau yn ffenest y gegin. Yna, cofiodd fod ei fam a'i dad wedi mynd â Siân, ei chwaer hŷn, i Gaer er mwyn dewis anrheg pen-blwydd iddi.

O, God! Dyna beth arall roedd o wedi anghofio ei wneud – prynu rhywbeth i Siân ar ei phen-blwydd. Medrai ei chlywed hi rŵan yn cwyno wrth iddo fo roi CD munud ola iddi. "Mae genna i hwn yn barod, Rhys. Dwi ddim yn gwybod pam nes di foddro." Hen fuwch sboilt oedd hi eniwe. Roedd ganddi hi bopeth yn barod.

Pan gyrhaeddodd Rhys y drws, medrai glywed Moss, y ci defaid, yn cyfarth yn wyllt o'r gegin. O leia roedd Moss yno i'w groesawu. Dyma Rhys yn rhoi'r goriad yn yr hen ddrws ffrynt a chlywodd glec wrth i Moss lamu at y drws. Y funud roedd y drws yn gilagored, roedd Moss yn bownsio rownd ac yn llyfu dwylo Rhys, â'i gynffon yn ysgwyd yn afreolus fel weipar car ar y sbîd cyflym.

Roedd y tŷ'n gynnes braf. Wedi i Rhys gynnau golau'r gegin, taflu ei fag ar y llawr a gadael Moss yn bwyta rhyw ŷd amryliw mewn hen bowlen frwnt wrth ddrws y cefn, rhoddodd ddŵr yn y tegell a dwy dafell o fara yn y tostiwr. Wrth i'r bara grasu a'r dŵr ddechrau berwi, safodd Rhys yn stond a syllu allan drwy ffenest y gegin gefn.

Wrth gwrs, doedd Durman ddim wedi gadael i

bethau fod ar ôl yr helynt yn y gwasanaeth. Neithiwr, roedd Rhys wedi bod ar ei draed tan ddau o'r gloch y bore yn sgwennu am gredoau atgyfodiad gwahanol grefyddau. Syniad hollol ddwl, ond roedd Mathew'n credu'n bendant bod pobol yn dod nôl yn fyw ar ôl marw. Wrth gwrs, roedd Mathew isio dod nôl fel yr *invisible man* er mwyn cael gwylio'r merched yn tynnu eu dillad yn y stafell newid cyn Chwaraeon. Wrth i Rhys estyn i godi sain y CD 'Smôcs, coffi a fodca rhad' gan Meinir Gwilym ar y system sain, dyma fo'n tollti coffi dros fwrdd y gegin a gwlychu ymylon ei draethawd. Roedd o wedi ei sychu ac wedi anghofio am y peth y funud y cyffyrddodd ei ben â gobennydd cwsg. Ond, yn y dosbarth y bore ma, roedd Durman wedi'i alw fo allan o flaen y dosbarth ac wedi taflu'r traethawd i'r bin o flaen pawb, "am mai dyna'r lle gorau i rybish."

Y tost yn neidio o'r tostiwr ddeffrodd Rhys o'i synfyfyrio ac, am ennyd, gwelodd adlewyrchiad ei wyneb yn ffenest y gegin. Edrychai'n welw.

Ar ôl taenu menyn hallt a haenen dew o fêl ar hyd y bara twym, eisteddodd Rhys wrth fwrdd y gegin gan fwrw cip ar y *Daily Post*. Ond methai â chanolbwyntio ar y geiriau du a gwyn. Roedd y tŷ'n dawel iawn. Dechreuodd Rhys rythu ar wyneb ceinciog y bwrdd. Yna, fe welodd y nodyn ac arno restr o bethau i'w gwneud. Hwfro, tacluso ei stafell, bwydo'r gwartheg, golchi llestri. Y cyfan cyn iddyn nhw ddod adre. Roedd Siân yn cael galifantio yng Nghaer. "Mam, fedra i ddim neud hynna heno, dwi'n mynd i'r practis côr... Dad, mae'n oer! Gaiff Rhys ei neud o?" Yr un fath bob tro. Wel stwffio gneud dim byd heno.

Dringodd Rhys i fyny'r grisiau. Medrai glywed clecian y gwres canolog a rhyw siffrwd disgwylgar yng nghorneli pellaf a thywyllaf y tŷ fel petai'r cysgodion yn gwrando arno wrth iddo droedio ar hyd carped y landin. Aeth i mewn i'w stafell wely a chau'r drws. Dyma lle roedd o'n teimlo'n saff, ynghanol ei bethe'i hun. Trodd Rhys at raglen gerddoriaeth ar y teledu bach a chodi'r sain yn uchel. Yna, taniodd y cyfrifiadur. Roedd clecian a gwichian rhyfedd y peiriant wrth iddo ddeffro, a'r hymian trydanol cynnes pan oedd o ar fynd yn llenwi'r stafell. Yn y sŵn cyson, cysurus, disgynnodd Rhys fel sach o datws ar ei wely. Trodd ar ei gefn a suddo i mewn i'r duvet cynnes.

'Pam na fedrai bywyd fod fel hyn o hyd?' meddyliodd wrth gwtsio yn y duvet cynnes, gwthio ei ddwylo dan y gobennydd i gorneli oer y fatras a chladdu ei ben yn y cwrlid meddal. Tasa fo'n byw ar ei ben ei hun, gallai aros yn y fan hyn yn gorwedd ar ei wely am byth.

Meddyliodd sut y base fo'n teimlo tase heddwas yn dod at y drws heno a deud, "Mae'n ddrwg iawn gen i, Mr Jones, ond mi fuo na ddamwain car, ac mae arna i ofn… " Oedi am ychydig… "bod eich teulu chi i gyd wedi'u lladd." Wrth gwrs y basa fo'n drist, ond wedyn galle fo neud fel licie fo. Mynd i nôl y gwn a saethu brain drwy'r dydd; cael partis gwyllt yn y tŷ drwy'r nos; byw yma hefo Helen Sharpe a chael digon o ryw. Fasa fo'n saethu'r gwartheg. Mynd i'r sied a'u saethu nhw'n farw wrth y cafn bwyd. *God*! Fasa hynna'n briliant! Hefyd, mi fasa fo'n gallu gwrando ar holl CDs ei chwaer. *God*! Hefyd, mi fasa fo'n gallu watsiad ffilmiau budur drwy'r nos, cael Mathew draw a...

Wel, *actually*, mi fasa'n reit neis gweld Mathew yn diodde am unwaith. Rhywbeth reit *embarassing*. Yn Gwaith Coed, mi fasa fo'n rhoid pen Mathew mewn feis a chau'r feis yn reit dynn am ei ben o. Wedyn, gofyn i bawb ddod mewn i'r stafell – pobol fel Helen, neu Nicola hwyrach, a gneud i Mathew grio o'u blaenau nhw wrth iddo fo dynhau'r feis. A deud y gwir, hwyrach y basa fo'n dal i gau'r feis nes bod penglog Mathew yn cracio. Neu hwyrach ddim.

Na, *hang on*, Durman ddylai ei chael hi. Rhaid cael rhywbeth rili arbennig i'r twat yna. Cael rhyw fath o *guillotine* a fo, Rhys, yn dal y cortyn a oedd yn rheoli cwymp y llafn. Cael Durman i sgrechian am faddeuant. Fasa'r mochyn dyn yn ymddiheuro am bopeth ac yn cyfadda ei fod o wedi bod yn fastad llwyr. Ond, mi fasa Rhys yn tynnu ar y cortyn run fath, a'r llafn yn cwympo a...

Na – rhy hawdd, rhy gyflym. Mi fasa angen bat *baseball* i waldio Durman, ei waldio fo nes ei fod o'n feddal ac yn waed i gyd.

Yn rhyfedd iawn, bob tro yr oedd yr athro Ysgrythur yn marw yn nrychfeddwl Rhys, roedd o'n ailgodi'n fyw eto – ond ei fod o bob amser yn fwy na'r tro cynt. Dechreuodd Rhys deimlo'n sâl wrth i neidr lawn llysnafedd ei feddwl ddechrau troi a throsi fel gwythïen ludiog ddu yn ei ben. Cododd yn sydyn ac edrych ar ei gyfrifiadur. Dim un e-bost. Roedd yn well iddo fo fynd i fwydo'r gwartheg neu fo fasa'n feddal pan ddychwelai ei dad o Gaer.

Camodd Rhys allan i'r noson oer â fflachlamp yn ei law, a dechreuodd gerdded i gyfeiriad sied y gwartheg. Lle'r oedd Moss, tybed? Ar ryw grwydr rywle yn y goedwig y tu ôl i'r tŷ, mae'n siŵr. Llithrodd follt y drws haearn yn ôl, camu i mewn i'r hongliad lle, a chwilio am y bwced fwyd yn y gornel. Roedd hi'n dawel iawn yno, heb ddim brefu na chwythu diamynedd. Be oedd yn bod ar y gwartheg? Cododd y fflachlamp a throi llif y golau i ben draw'r sied. Dyna lle roeddan nhw'n swatio'n ffurfiau tywyll, tywyll. Od iawn. Penderfynodd Rhys beidio â'u bwydo heno. Teimlai'n rhyfedd yno. Camodd nôl wysg ei gefn at y drws, a bwrw stôl wrth wneud hynny. Rhedodd nôl at y tŷ. Câi Siân fwydo'r blincin anifeiliaid pan ddôi hi adre.

Aeth Rhys nôl i'w stafell wely a chau'r drws ar ei ôl. Blymin gwartheg gwirion! Eisteddodd ar ei wely a tshecio ei e-bost. Un. 'Mathew Creed'! Be ddiawl oedd ar hwn isio rŵan? Agorodd yr e-bost. Roedd *attachment* efo'r neges – clip fideo oddi ar y we. Agorodd Rhys yr *attachment*.

Am eiliad, doedd o ddim yn deall be roedd o'n ei weld. Mathew oedd o, ond roedd rhywbeth dros bob rhan o'i ben. Jam, sôs coch... ? Be gythraul oedd o wedi bod yn ei neud? Roedd llygaid Mathew ar agor led y pen ac roedd y siâp mwyaf od ar ei wyneb. Ac roedd ei lais yn od.

"Rhys... Rhys... " A dyna fo. Daeth y neges i ben. Cês!

Cododd ei ffôn symudol a ffonio Mathew. Be oedd yn bod arno fo, y diawl gwirion?

"Helo, pwy sy 'na?" meddai'r llais y pen arall.

Chwarddodd Rhys. "Ga i chwech *pizza* a photel o biso cath, plîs?"

"Pwy sy na?" Llais diarth.

"George Bush, ac mae'n rhaid imi gael dynas ar frys... " Meddwl. "Mat? Mat?"

"Gwrandwch. Heddwas ydw i. Dwi yn nhŷ Mathew Creed. Pwy sy'n siarad?"

"Rhys Jones, ffrind Mathew."

"Reit, gwranda, mae Mathew wedi bod mewn rhyw fath o ddamwain yn gynharach heddiw. Be ydy dy gyfeiriad di? Rhif ffôn?"

"Be sy di digwydd?" gofynnodd Rhys. Medrai glywed sgrechian gwraig yn y cefndir y tu ôl i lais yr heddwas.

"Mi ddown ni i dy weld di fory, Rhys."

Wrth siarad ar y ffôn, roedd Rhys wedi bod yn edrych yn ddifeddwl ar sgrîn y teledu. Yn sydyn, fe wawriodd arno – llun o'r dre ar y newyddion; llun o'r ysgol! Diffoddodd ei ffôn ac ymbalfalu'n wyllt am y teclyn i godi'r sain. Clywodd y geiriau, "lle y digwyddodd ymosodiad ffyrnig yn gynharach heddiw... Mae'r heddlu'n bryderus iawn am ddiogelwch un o'r athrawon, Mr Elfyn Durman, pum deg a phedair oed. Does neb wedi gweld Mr Durman ers chwech o'r gloch heno, ac mae'r heddlu'n pwysleisio bod angen gofal ysbyty arno... "

Diffoddodd Rhys y teledu. Medrai glywed rhyw sŵn curo od. Gwrandawodd, a sylweddoli mai ei galon oedd yn dyrnu curo yn ei fynwes.

Gorweddodd yn ôl ar ei wely a chraffu ar y craciau yn nenfwd yr ystafell. Edrychodd i bob cornel. Byddai gwneud hynny fel arfer yn llonyddu ei feddwl, ond, rŵan, fedrai o wneud dim i dawelu curiad ei galon. Roedd yn llenwi'r ystafell, y tŷ a'r cwm.

Yn araf, dechreuodd cysgod melyn gripio ar hyd nenfwd y stafell. Yna, sŵn car yn dod i lawr y ffordd. Diolch byth – ei fam a'i dad! Cododd Rhys a rhedeg lawr y staer, ddau ris ar y tro, ac allan i'r buarth. Gallai weld y car yn dod i lawr y ffordd at y tŷ.

Ond roedd rhywbeth yn bod ar y car. Roedd y goleuadau'n pwyntio i ddau gyfeiriad gwahanol. Nhw oedd yno: sŵn y Peugeot oedd o, er bod yr injian yn swnio'n od braidd. Wrth i'r car agosáu, gwelodd Rhys fod ei do'n edrych yn rhyfedd. Yn isel, rywsut. Yn rhy isel.

Cyrhaeddodd y car y buarth a stopio gyda'r un golau oedd yn dal i wynebu mlaen yn dallu Rhys. Roedd y golau arall yn anelu i fyny i'r awyr. Roedd y car wedi malu, a thrwy ei ffenestri gallai weld ei fam a'i dad a Siân yn rhythu'n fud arno. Yna, gyda sgrech fetalaidd, agorodd un o ddrysau'r car a chamodd ffurf allan. Ond roedd yn cael trafferth cerdded yn iawn – roedd yn hercian o flaen llifolau'r car, a doedd ganddo ddim rheolaeth dros ei freichiau.

Rhuthrodd Rhys nôl i'r tŷ. Caeodd y drws ffrynt. A bolltio'r drws – y top a'r gwaelod...

Un funud fach...
gan Rocet Arwel Jones

Fedrai o? Roedd o wedi breuddwydio am yr eiliad hon ers wythnosau. Wrth ei waith bob dydd, wrth fynd i'r gwasanaeth bob dydd Sul, cyn mynd i gysgu, roedd o wedi breuddwydio am yr eiliad hon. Ond fedrai o? Roedd o'n sefyll yno â'r gwn yn dynn wrth dalcen y cachgi o'i flaen nes bod y croen o gwmpas y baril yn gylch gwyn. Ond a fedrai o dynnu'r glicied?

Ambell eiliad roedd llygaid y llofrudd o'i flaen yn neidio'n ôl a blaen mewn ofn ac yn chwilio am ryw obaith yn rhywle. A'r eiliad nesaf roeddent wedi rhewi'n byllau glas, llonydd, yn syllu i lawr y baril i fyw llygaid Math – yn erfyn am ei fywyd, ac yn chwilio am wendid, am faddeuant, am gydymdeimlad.

Roedd o'n haeddu marw – yn araf a phoenus. Dyna oedd Math wedi'i gynllunio. Ei anafu yn ei goes, gwneud yn siŵr ei fod o'n taro gwythïen ddigon mawr, a'i adael yno i farw'n ara ac i feddwl am yr hyn roedd o wedi'i wneud. Dyna oedd o'n ei haeddu. Dyna fyddai cyfiawnder. Dyna fyddai dial teg. Ond a fedrai o dynnu'r glicied?

Wrth edrych i fyny oddi ar y llawr, roedd y llofrudd yn dychmygu ei fod o'n gweld mymryn o ansicrwydd yn llygaid Math o dro i dro, rhyw gymylau meddal o gydymdeimlad, ond cyn pen dim roedd rheiny'n rhewi'n gasineb caled. Ai dyma fyddai'i ddiwedd – gorwedd yng nghornel hen ffermdy anghysbell, ei ymennydd fel darnau o bizza yn glynu wrth y wal tu ôl iddo? Efallai mai dyna oedd o'n ei haeddu am yr hyn roedd o wedi'i wneud. Ond o leia fe fyddai'n marw'n arwr – fel un a roddodd ei fywyd dros yr achos. Fe fyddai ei dad a'i frodyr yn dial am ei lofruddiaeth. Rhaid i bob milwr fod yn barod, ac roedd o'n barod. Pam na fyddai o'n tanio'r gwn ac yn dod â'r cyfan i ben?

Oedd yr anifail ar ben arall y gwn yn gallu teimlo'r cryndod yn ei law? Oedd o'n crynu neu ai dim ond fo oedd yn dychmygu'r cyfan? Roedd Math yn syllu mor galed i lawr baril y gwn nes ei fod o'n methu â gweld dim. Doedd dim ond duwch o'i flaen ac, yn y duwch hwnnw, roedd ei atgofion yn rhuthro fel fideo gwallgo o'r chwith i'r dde...

Teimlo Hannah yn gafael yn dynn am ei goes. Prin ei bod hi'n gallu cerdded. Gafael am ei goes fel y byddai llanciau'r pentre yn gafael yn ddiog am bolyn lamp. Roedd hi mor fychan. Dibynnu'n llwyr arno fo, Math, ei brawd. Fo oedd ei chadernid. Roedd y ffaith ei bod yn dibynnu arno yn gwneud iddo deimlo'n falch, yn gryf. Roedd hi'n ymddiried ynddo. Yr eiliad honno y sylweddolodd gymaint roedd yn ei charu hi – y chwaer fach roedd o wedi bod yn eithaf cenfigennus ohoni, y ferch fach roedd o wedi gorfod rhannu ei rieni gyda hi ar ôl un mlynedd ar ddeg o fod yn unig blentyn. Yr eiliad honno y sylweddolodd y byddai wedi rhoi ei fywyd drosti hi. Roedd hi â'i chwrls melyn yno yn chwarae mig gyda Jo ei ffrind gorau. Roedd hi'n gyfarwydd â Jo, ond ddim yn ddigon cyfarwydd i ymddiried ynddo fel roedd hi'n ymddiried yn ei brawd mawr. Roedd ei llygaid glas yn chwerthin yn braf wrth i Jo esgus chwilio amdani ymhobman ac wedyn dod o hyd iddi yn cuddio yng nghôl Math.

Dyddiau braf oedd y dyddiau cyn yr helyntion, cyn y casineb. Dyddiau'r chwerthin a'r gwenu, dyddiau o esgus chwarae â gynnau, dyddiau o esgus marw – rhesi o gyrff ymhobman yn gwingo gan chwerthin ac yn marw â gwên ar eu hwynebau.

Bu Hannah farw â gwên ar ei hwyneb. Y wên fwya direidus. Yr un wên â honno a oedd ar ei hwyneb wrth i Jo esgus chwilio amdani yn y caffi. Chwerthin yn ofnus, ond yn gwybod yn iawn ei bod yn ddiogel, yn gwybod nad oedd dim yn y byd yn mynd i beri niwed iddi tra byddai'n gafael yn dynn yng nghoes ei brawd. Dyna'r wên a oedd ar ei hwyneb, ond bod y wên yn llonydd, y llygaid glas wedi troi'n llwyd a'i bywyd yn bwll bach o waed ar y pafin wrth ei hymyl. Cyn lleied o waed oedd yn ei chorff bychan.

Pam nad oedd o yno i'w gwarchod? Pam bu'n rhaid iddi fynd i'r dre hefo'u hewyrth a'u modryb? Fyddai dim byd

wedi peri niwed iddi tra byddai o yno i'w hamddiffyn. Ond doedd o ddim yno. Roedd o allan yn chwilio am gêm o bêl-droed.

Heddiw, dyma fo wedi dod o hyd i'w llofrudd. Y person a ddygodd fywyd ei chwaer fach. Roedd o ar ben draw'r baril ac roedd o'n mynd i dalu. Roedd gan Math gymaint i'w ddweud, cymaint roedd o am ei ofyn. Roedd o am weiddi ond roedd o'n cael trafferth sibrwd. Roedd o am regi ond roedd o'n fud. Gwyliodd bry cop yn dringo gweddillion y papur wal ar ei ffordd yn ôl i'w we. Roedd y papur ar y wal wedi ei dynnu rywsut rywsut, a rhwyg blêr tebyg i fynyddoedd ar y gorwel ar ei ôl. A'r pry cop yn brasgamu fel anghenfil anferth o fynydd i fynydd. Deffrodd Math o'i synfyfyrio a chwipiodd ei lygaid yn ôl at ei elyn fel petai tynnu ei lygaid oddi arno yn ddigon iddo fedru dianc.

Aeth eiliadau hir heibio a'r distawrwydd fel petai'n gwthio'r ddau yn nes ac yn nes at ei gilydd. Taniodd gwn yn y pellter a pheri iddyn nhw neidio. Yn sydyn, roedd sŵn curiad calon y ddau yn llenwi'r ystafell. Yna, distawrwydd, a'r distawrwydd yn cael ei dorri gan sŵn gêm bêl-droed rywle yn y pellter. Bechgyn yn mwynhau eu hunain a bywyd bob dydd yn blaguro eto yng nghanol yr helyntion.

Dyna lle'r oedd Math wedi bod y diwrnod hwnnw. Wedi bod yn chwilio am ffrindiau i weld a oedd rhywun yn barod i ddod i chwarae pêl-droed. Curodd ar ddrws pawb, ond roedd pawb yn brysur. Mentrodd draw i'r pentre nesa i chwilio am Jo. Taflodd gerrig at ei ffenest yn ôl ei arfer, ond doedd dim sôn amdano.

Roedd Jo a Math wedi bod yn ffrindiau ers pan oedden nhw'n blant bach. Wedi eu geni yn yr un pentre, ar yr un diwrnod, er nad yn yr un ysbyty. Math am wyth o'r gloch y bore, a Jo bob amser yn mynnu ei fod wedi ei eni cyn hynny. Math, felly, oedd wedi ei eni yr un diwrnod ag o. Ond gwyddai Math ym mêr ei esgyrn mai fo oedd yr hyna, ac roedd hynny'n bwysig pan oeddech chi'n ddeg oed! Roedden nhw'n efeilliaid, a dyna oedd yn bwysig. Ond, er eu bod nhw'n efeilliaid, yn allanol, doedden nhw ddim yn edrych yn debyg i'w gilydd. Roedd Math yn dal ac yn gryf ac yn dywyll o ran pryd a gwedd, gyda chroen euraidd, gwallt hir du fel y frân a llygaid tywyll, tywyll. Roedd Jo yr un mor gryf ond yn stwcyn llydan caled, gyda chroen golau, llygaid glas a gwallt cringoch pigog. Ond ar y tu mewn, roedden nhw'r un ffunud – yn eneidiau hoff cytun.

Am flynyddoedd, doedd dim modd gwahanu'r ddau. Mynd i bobman gyda'i gilydd a gwneud popeth gyda'i gilydd. Rhannu pob cyfrinach, a doedd dim angen i'r naill dynnu sylw'r llall at rywbeth doniol. Byddai edrych ar ei gilydd yn ddigon ac yna chwerthin yn afreolus. Fyddai neb arall yn gwybod beth oedd i gyfri am y fath hwyl, ac fe ddechreuodd rhai pobl feddwl bod y ddau'n seicic!

Pêl-droed oedd eu dileit mawr, ac roedd y ddau'n bartneriaid perffaith wrth ymosod. Doedd dim rhaid i'r un ohonyn nhw weiddi am y bêl nac edrych i weld a oedd y llall yno cyn pasio; roedden nhw'n gwybod yn reddfol lle i sefyll. Doedd dim gwahaniaeth pwy oedd yn sgorio; unwaith roedd y bêl yng nghefn y rhwyd, byddai'r ddau'n taflu eu breichiau am ei gilydd ac yn moesymgrymu i'r dorf ddychmygol, fel pe na byddai neb arall yn y tîm.

Doedd pethau ddim mor hawdd wedi i'r helyntion ddechrau. Roedd yn rhaid iddyn nhw chwarae i dimau gwahanol. Doedd Math ddim yn cael chwarae i'r un tîm ag un o'u plant Nhw. Ond llwyddodd y bechgyn barhau i chwarae pêl-droed bob prynhawn, er bod eu teuluoedd yn gwgu. Roedd y teuluoedd yn fodlon diodde'n dawel cyn belled â bod dau dîm a bod y bechgyn yn chwarae'n erbyn ei gilydd. Fe fyddai'r ddau'n chwarae'n galed ar y cae pêl-droed – a hyd yn oed yn ymladd unwaith neu ddwy – ac yn gweiddi a rhegi ar ei gilydd, y naill a'r llall yn ei iaith ei hun. Ond, wedi'r gêm, roedd y ddau mor agos ag erioed. Doedd wiw i Math, serch hynny, gael ei ddal yn mynd at ddrws ffrynt tŷ Jo. Byddai'n sleifio heibio'r ci cysglyd wrth y drws cefn ac yn taflu cerrig at ffenest Jo, a byddai yntau'n dod allan cyn gynted ag y medrai wneud esgus.

Ond doedd neb o gwmpas y prynhawn hwnnw. Pe na byddai o wedi mynd i chwilio am fechgyn y pentre ac wedi aros i warchod Hannah, fyddai hi ddim wedi cael ei lladd.

A dyma fo wedi dal y sawl a oedd yn gyfrifol, a hwnnw'n gwingo ar lawr o'i flaen. Tynhaodd ei afael ar y glicied. Un symudiad bychan bach ac fe fyddai bywyd y gelyn hwn ar ben. Y symudiad lleia posib. Symudiad na fyddai modd ei weld hyd yn oed. Roedd y glicied yn dynn a'i darged yn sicr. Dim ond tynnu ei fys y mymryn lleia ac fe fyddai'r cyfan ar ben. Ar ben... neu ar fin dechrau?

Synhwyrodd y llofrudd fod gafael tynnach ar y gwn wrth ei ben erbyn hyn. Pam na fyddai'n tynnu'r glicied? Am faint y buon nhw'n sefyll yma fel hyn? Oriau? Roedd dychmygu'r hyn a oedd ar fin digwydd yn waeth na'r digwyddiad ei hun. Dychmygu'r glec, y boen, a'r bywyd yn llifo ohono. Y cyfan yn dod i ben.

Byth ers iddo gyrraedd adre y prynhawn hwnnw, â'i deulu wedi ei chwalu a chorff ei chwaer ym mreichiau ei dad, roedd Math wedi treulio pob awr o'r dydd yn chwilio am lofrudd ei chwaer. Rhaid mai dyn yn byw'n lleol oedd o. Roedd gan bob teulu waed ar eu dwylo. Pawb wedi colli rhywun, a phawb yn cuddio rhyw derfysgwr neu lofrudd o dan domen flêr o dawelwch a chelwydd. O wrando'n ddigon astud, byddai'n siŵr o glywed pwy laddodd ei chwaer. Dyna natur yr helyntion – roedd rhai cyfrinachau'n gyfrinachau agored.

Bu'n chwilio'n ddyfal, ac, ar y cychwyn, cafodd gymorth ei gyfeillion pêl-droed. Galwodd bob un yn eu tro i gydymdeimlo. Pob un yn anghyfforddus yn y tawelwch annifyr, yn llonydd ac yn dawel ac yn ysgwyd dwylo fel hen ddynion. Yn eistedd heb allu edrych i lygaid neb. Cyrhaeddodd Jo ar y trydydd diwrnod â golwg ofnadwy arno. Roedd Math wedi bod yn meddwl lle'r oedd o wedi bod. Ei ffrind gorau, a dim sôn amdano. Ond mae'n siŵr nad oedd pethau'n hawdd dan yr amgylchiadau. Pan gyrhaeddodd, gallai Math fod wedi taeru mai Jo ei hun oedd wedi colli ei chwaer. Yn welw ac yn flêr, roedd golwg fel petai heb gysgu ers dyddiau arno. Roedd gan Jo gymaint o feddwl o Hannah nes ei bod hi fel chwaer iddo yntau hefyd. Roedden nhw wedi treulio cymaint o amser gyda'i gilydd, ac roedd yntau, fel Math, wedi bod o gwmpas i'w gweld hi'n tyfu.

Pawb yn dod i gydymdeimlo a phawb yn sôn am ddial arnyn Nhw, ond doedd gan neb syniad eto pwy'n union oedd wedi gwneud. Pawb yn addo chwilio. Ambell un yn ffansïo'i hun fel rhyw James Bond yn rhedeg yma ac acw yn holi hwn a'r llall ac yn bygwth bechgyn eraill – rhai llai na nhw eu hunain fel arfer. Ond roedd gan y rhan fwya dacteg fwy effeithiol wrth iddyn nhw eistedd gartre a gwrando ar y teulu'n siarad. Eistedd yn dawel a llonydd gan guddio tu ôl i lyfr a chlustfeinio ar bob sibrydiad. Gwenu wrth wrando ar oedolion yn siarad mewn iaith ffug yn y gobaith nad oedd y plant yn eu deall. A hwythau'n deall pob gair ers blynyddoedd! Ond chlywodd neb ddim byd. Doedd hyd yn oed Jo ddim wedi clywed unrhyw beth ac yntau'n un ohonyn Nhw. Roedd popeth yn dawel fel y bedd.

Ar ôl peth amser, peidiodd yr adrodd yn ôl, a marwolaeth Hannah yn cael ei gwthio o'r sgwrs gan ffrwydrad arall a marwolaeth arall. Roedd pawb wedi colli rhywun. Ond roedd Math wedi colli Hannah, a doedd o ddim wedi anghofio. Doedd o ddim yn teimlo fel chwarae pêl-droed, ac, felly, mewn caffis myglyd yn gwylio'r byd yn prysuro heibio y byddai o. Doedd o ddim wedi gweld yr un o'i gyfeillion ers dyddiau – roedd pawb wedi mynd yn ddieithr iawn. Dyna ei gosb am fethu â thalu'r pwyth yn ôl am farwolaeth ei chwaer fach.

Roedd yn eistedd mewn caffi un prynhawn, yn boddi yn ei atgofion ac yn toddi'n un â'r paent melyn budur ar y wal, pan glywodd ddau ddyn yn siarad. Yn eu hanner Nhw o'r caffi roedden nhw'n eistedd. Mewn eiliad dawel ynghanol y clebran, a glywodd o'n iawn? Ddeallodd o'r hyn a glywodd o? Oedd y ddau hen ddyn yn trafod ei chwaer fach o? Glywodd o un yn dweud wrth y llall fod llofrudd y ferch fach benfelen honno yn cuddio mewn hen ffermdy ar ochr y mynydd? Tybed?

Am y tro cyntaf ers wythnosau, pwmpiodd yr adrenalin trwy gorff Math. Bron nad oedd o'n teimlo'n hapus, yn teimlo fel chwerthin a gweiddi a rhuthro o dŷ i dŷ, yn cyhoeddi'r newyddion da. Ond pwyllodd. Cododd a cherdded allan. Roedd ganddo gynllun. Dyma gyfle i weithredu. Gwelodd ei dad yn dangos i'w fam droeon sut i ddefnyddio'r gwn, a hynny er mwyn iddi allu ei hamddiffyn ei hun, heb feddwl bod y bachgen yn y gornel â'i ben yn ei lyfr yn gwrando ar bob gair, ac yn gwylio.

Roedd ei gartre'n wag. Cerddodd yn dawel i ystafell ei rieni ac agor y cwpwrdd wrth ochr y gwely. Teimlo cymysgedd o chwilfrydedd ac euogrwydd wrth chwalu drwy bethau personol ei fam. Pethau ei fam oedden nhw, ei gofod bach preifat hi ei hun, ac yng nghefn y gofod hwn, wedi ei guddio a'i lapio mewn hen glwt, roedd y gwn a'r bwledi. Cododd y gwn a'i osod ym mhoced ei gôt cyn cychwyn am yr hen ffermdy.

Ar y ffordd, penderfynodd alw am Jo. Er nad oedd wedi ei weld ers wythnosau, roedd o'n gwybod y byddai Jo am fod yn rhan o hyn. Taflodd gerrig mân at y ffenest, ond doedd dim ateb. Roedd y tŷ'n wag ac yn rhyfedd o dawel. Wrth iddo adael yr ardd, clywodd y ci'n rhuthro o rywle gan chwyrnu a chyfarth a brathu wrth ei sodlau. Roedd y ci'n arfer bod mor addfwyn. Beth oedd wedi digwydd? Prysurodd yn ei flaen a'r ci'n cyfarth yn wyllt ar ymyl y ffin anweledig a farciai ei batsh ei hun.

Anghofiodd am y ci ac am Jo wrth frasgamu allan o'r pentre am y mynydd. Gyda phob cam o'r daith, aeth dros bob symudiad yn y broses. Yr holi a'r cyhuddo, y gweiddi a'r rhegi, y saethu, a'r pwll o waed. Gwaed y sawl a laddodd ei chwaer. Roedd y cyfan ar fin dod i ben – yr wythnosau o gynllunio'r dial a'r lladd, a'r meddyliau'n troi yn ei ben fel dillad mewn peiriant golchi nes bod y cyfan yn pwyso arno'n gwlwm trwm. Wrth i'r ffermdy ddod i'r golwg, a thyfu'n fwy ac yn fwy wrth iddo nesáu, gwyddai'n reddfol bod ei elyn rhwng ei bedair wal.

Arafodd am eiliad cyn camu i mewn i'r tŷ. Doedd dim drws yno. Chwiliodd ym mhob ystafell ar y llawr gwaelod yn gyflym ac yn dawel, ond doedd dim sôn am neb. Dringodd y grisiau. Fferrodd wrth iddyn nhw wichian. Pe bai rhywun yno, a gwn ganddo, byddai'n disgwyl amdano a byddai ar ben arno. Ond doedd dim troi'n ôl. Mentrodd symud, ei wn o'i flaen yn barod i saethu. Crwydrodd yn araf o'r naill ystafell i'r llall heb ddod ar draws neb. Gwelodd ddrws ym mhen draw'r ystafell fwyaf, a oedd, yn amlwg, yn arwain at ystafell arall. Os oedd unrhyw un yn cuddio, yn y fan hyn byddai o.

Gafaelodd ym mwlyn y drws. Roedd pob gewyn yn ei gorff yn dynn. Troi. Pob blewyn ar ei ben yn sefyll yn stond, yn gwrando ac yn teimlo. Hon oedd yr eiliad roedd o wedi breuddwydio cymaint amdani. Teimlo'r drws yn ildio o filimedr i filimedr. Anadlu'n ddwfn cyn troi'r bwlyn yn gyflym a rhuthro i mewn i'r ystafell.

"Be ddiawl wyt ti'n da yma?"

Ac wrth holi'r cwestiwn am yr ail dro, fe wawriodd y gwirionedd arno.

"Jo! Be wyt ti'n da yma?"

Gwyddai'r ateb. Gwyddai rŵan pam bod Jo'n edrych mor ofnadwy pan alwodd i gydymdeimlo.

Gwyddai pam nad oedd o wedi gweld ei ffrind ers cymaint o amser. Gwyddai pam bod y tŷ'n wag a'r ci mor filain. Y fo, Jo, oedd wedi lladd Hannah.

"Y bastad!!!"

Rhuthrodd ato a dal y gwn at ei ben. Wnaeth o ddim ymladd, dim ond eistedd yno'n llonydd â'i lygaid yn llawn ofn ac ansicrwydd.

"Pam? Pam? Hannah, o bawb. Chdi o bawb. Pam? Sut? Saethu merch fach ddiniwed? Roedd hi'n meddwl y byd ohonat ti? Roeddat ti fel brawd iddi. Y bastad! Pam? Pam?"

"Doeddwn i… ddim… wedi… bwriadu… " Teimlai Math bob gair yn cropian yn grynedig fesul un i fyny baril y gwn wrth i Jo agor ei geg i siarad am y tro cynta.

"Ddim wedi bwriadu? Ddim wedi bwriadu? Roeddat ti'n digwydd bod yn cerdded i lawr y stryd, yn digwydd bod yn cario gwn, ac fe ddigwyddaist ti saethu?!"

"Doeddwn i ddim wedi bwriadu saethu Hannah. Dy ewyrth oedd y targed. Fo laddodd fy nghefnder y gaea diwetha. Mi nath y gell 'y newis i i ddial. Y job gynta ges i. Roedd o'n haeddu… "

"Ond fe laddist ti Hannah… "

"Roedd yn rhaid dial. Doedd dim dewis. Roedd yn rhaid dial. Roedd yn rhaid gwneud fel roedden nhw'n ddweud. Roedd yn rhaid i mi."

Allai Math ddim dweud yr un gair. Roedd y sgript wedi newid, y cymeriadau yn y ddrama wedi newid, ac yntau wedi bod yn ei hymarfer cyhyd. Roedd o'n casáu'r anifail y pen arall i faril y gwn. Ei ffrind gorau.

Yn ystod yr eiliad hir hon hyd yn oed, roedd o'n gwybod yn union beth oedd yn mynd trwy feddwl Math. Gwybod faint oedd o'n caru Hannah. Gwybod ei fod o'n gallu bod yn ffyrnig a phenderfynol ar gae pêl-droed. Gwybod nad oedd o'n newid ei feddwl ar ôl penderfynu ar dacl. Ond, eto, gwybod nad oedd o'n llofrudd.

Roedd Math hefyd yn gwybod nad oedd y Jo go-iawn yn gallu lladd. Yr helyntion uffernol a oedd wedi troi Jo'n llofrudd.

Ond roedd o wedi penderfynu. Roedd rhaid cyflawni'r hyn roedd o wedi'i addo i'w chwaer drwy gaead yr arch wen fechan a fu'n llenwi'r tŷ am dridiau hir rai misoedd yn gynt. Caeodd ei lygaid a gafael yn dynnach yn y gwn. Teimlo pwysau'r glicied yn ildio flewyn wrth flewyn. Y morthwyl yn barod i daro'r bwled drwy ben ei gyfaill. Meddwl am Hannah yn haul canol dydd â'i chorff bychan mor oer. Gwasgu fymryn ymhellach. Meddwl am ei fam yn crio bob nos a'i dad yn gafael yn dynn, dynn am wddw'r botel wisgi wrth ddrachtio ohoni. Gwasgu fymryn ymhellach eto.

Agorodd ei lygaid a theimlo'r dagrau yn llosgi ei fochau. Roedd llygaid Jo ar gau hefyd, yn disgwyl y diwedd. Meddwl am deulu Jo – ei frodyr a'i chwiorydd, ei dad penboeth a'i fam benderfynol. Meddwl am fechgyn y pentre. Faint ohonyn nhw a fyddai'n dial arno am ladd Jo a faint fyddai'n cadw ei gefn? Dychmygu aelodau'r tîm pêl-droed yn saethu at ei gilydd a phob un yn gorff marw ar lawr. Edrychodd ar y wyneb roedd o'n ei adnabod mor dda – y wyneb roedd o wedi ei weld yn newid wrth i'r ddau ohonyn nhw dyfu – a chofiodd y wên a'r chwerthin cyfarwydd.

Pan glywodd Jo y sŵn, saethodd ei lygaid led y pen ar agor. Oedd Math wedi methu ac yntau'n sefyll mor agos? Na. Roedd Mathew wedi taflu'r gwn yn erbyn y wal ac roedd yn sefyll yno'n llonydd, yn syllu ar Jo â'i lygaid yn gymysgfa gymhleth o siom, rhyddhad, tosturi, casineb ac ansicrwydd.

Cerddodd y ddau o'r ystafell gan adael y gwn ar lawr yn y gornel. I lawr y grisiau yn araf a sigledig ac allan i haul diwedd y prynhawn. Gwahanu a cherdded i gyfeiriadau gwahanol, y naill i'r dde a'r llall i'r chwith, heb ddweud yr un gair wrth ei gilydd.

Syrffio mewn cariad
gan Pryderi Gwyn Jones

"Llgada Sgwâr! Llgada Sgwâr!"

Agorodd Neil 'Llgada Sgwâr' Owen ei lygaid ac edrych ar y poster mawr o dîm Wrecsam oedd ar nenfwd ei ystafell wely. Nina, ei chwaer fach oedd yno yn gweiddi arno y peth cynta yn y bore unwaith eto. Roedd hi'n dew fel mwd ac yn pwyso mwy na fo er ei bod hi bedair blynedd yn iau. Roedd hi'n ddeg oed rŵan ac yn pwyso stôn am bob blwyddyn o'i bywyd.

"Iawn! Ocê! Mi goda i yn munud, pwdin," medda fo'n gysglyd i gyd.

"Ond dw i isio ti godi rŵan! Rŵan!"

"Pam?"

"Mae Mam wedi cuddio'r potyn *chocolate spread* yng nghefn y cwpwrdd eto ac fedra i mo'i gyrraedd."

"Dydy hi ddim isio i ti ei fwyta fo, nachdi, lwmpyn."

Dechreuodd ei chwer fach (fawr) wylltio'n gacwn wedyn. Nid am fod ei brawd mawr (bach) yn galw enwau arni ond am ei bod hi bron â marw eisiau'r *chocolate spread*. Roedd ei thost hi'n barod yn y gegin, ac yn oeri ac yn caledu ar y plât.

"O, plîs, Llgada Sgwâr. Mi wna i dost i ti fyd."

"A golchi llestri brecwast?" medda Llgada Sgwâr, yn meddwl sawl bargen y gallai ei chael gan ei chwaer.

"Iawn – tost a golchi llestri. Ond tyd yn dy flaen..."

Sbonciodd Llgada Sgwâr o'i wely, rhoi ei draed yn ei slipars, a bwrw golwg sydyn ar ei *Inbox*. Dwy neges newydd. Un e-bost gan Dyl ei gefnder yn malu awyr am ei foto-beic sgramblo newydd... ac, oedd, roedd 'na un neges fach ganddi Hi hefyd – dim ond yn dweud, 'BORE DA. DEL.'

Anfonodd neges yn ôl ati'n syth bin.

Message. Reply. 'BORE DA. AR FRYS – DIM AMSER I SGWRSIO NEU MI FYDDA I'N HWYR I'R YSGOL. GAWN NI AIR AMSER CINIO A MIN NOS. LLAWER O SWSUS, NEIL.'

Pan gyrhaeddodd y gegin, roedd Nina'n taenu menyn dros ddarn o dost.

"Dyna chdi. Mi gei di yr un yma. Fi pia'r ddau yn y tostiwr."

Estynnodd Neil y *chocolate spread* iddi.

"A'i agor o, cofia. Mae o wedi cael ei gau yn rhy dynn i mi."

"Iawn."

Sglaffiodd Neil y tost yn reit sydyn, er ei fod o wedi oeri ac ychydig bach yn galed. Dim ots, meddyliodd, fe lenwodd dwll. Roedd ganddo biti dros ei chwaer weithia; doedd hi ddim yn cael pwdin go-iawn run fath â chwstard neu *blancmange* yn yr ysgol – dim ond afal neu fanana – a dyna pam ei bod hi'n stwffio'i bol efo'r sothach brown 'na ar ei thost bob bore wedi i'w fam a'i dad fynd i'w gwaith.

"A penny for your thoughts, young man," medda Mrs Ramsbottom, yr athrawes Saesneg, wrth weld Neil yn syllu trwy ffenast y dosbarth a golwg bell, bell arno.

"Pwy – fi?" medda Neil wedi i Ifan B roi cic iddo fo dan y bwrdd.

"Yes – you. And do I have to remind you that English is the language to be spoken here in the English classroom in my English lesson?"

Oedd hi'n disgwyl ateb ta be?

"Yes, Miss. I mean – no, Miss."

"What on earth is wrong with you, boy? You have lost your concentration. I dare say my goldfish could keep his mind on a task longer than you. Now, pay attention, or you will never understand the importance of Banquo in this particular scene."

Dyna'r trydydd pryd o dafod iddo'i gael yr wythnos hon. Roedd hyn yn dechra mynd yn beth cyffredin, a doedd hynny ddim yn beth da. Mi gafodd o ffrae gan Jones Gym echdoe am fod fel rhech yn y wers griced – byth yn cadw'i lygad ar y bêl, medda hwnnw, a bod yn rhaid gwneud hynny neu fe alla fo gael ei daro ar dop ei drwyn, a hyn a'r llall ac arall... Mi gafodd ram-dam gan

Mrs Ellis, Cerddoriaeth, hefyd am syllu ar noda ei allweddella yn lle chwarae'r hyn roedd o wedi'i gyfansoddi. Arni Hi roedd y bai. Hi, a neb arall. Byth ers iddo ei chyfarfod Hi ar y we doedd 'na ddim byd arall wedi bod ar ei feddwl. Allai o ddim peidio â meddwl amdani – roedd Hi'n llenwi ei feddwl o nos a dydd.

Ond nid Neil Llgada Sgwâr oedd yr unig un â'i feddwl yn bell. Nid fo oedd yr unig un ag adar bach yn canu'n ei ben a'r haul yn goleuo'i fyd bob dydd er gwaetha'r glaw a gurai ar ffenestri'r ysgol bob bore a phnawn.

"Be sy'n bod arnat ti, Ifan B?" gofynnodd i'w ffrind gora.

"Dim byd," medda hwnnw, yn gwenu fel giât a'i lygaid yn edrych i rywle na welai neb arall.

"Ond ti'n dy fyd bach dy hun ac yn ddistaw – yn deud dim wrth neb."

"Chdi sy'n meddwl. Dw i'n iawn, siŵr."

"Ond ti'n wahanol."

"Ti'n un da i ddeud. Ti'm yn chdi dy hun chwaith. Mae'r athrawon hyd yn oed di sylwi – heb sôn amdana i a'r hogia, dallta di."

"Wel, dw inna'n iawn hefyd. Meddwl am y gemau newydd 'na dw di anfon amdanyn nhw dw i, a dim byd arall."

Doedd Neil erioed wedi bod yn un da am ddeud

celwydd. Ond ddywedodd Ifan B ddim, dim ond sbïo run fath â llo, gafael yn ei fag a hel ei draed am y wers nesa.

Roedd yn rhaid iddo fynd i'r stafell gyfrifiaduron amser cinio. Roedd o wedi addo cysylltu efo HI y bore hwnnw, yn doedd? Byddai'n rhaid iddo feddwl am esgus os oedd o am fynd heibio Edwyn IT, y technegydd oedd yn edrych ar ôl y lle drwy gydol yr awr ginio. Anghofiodd am ei ginio a cherddodd yn syth i stafell 23. Roedd Edwyn yno yn ôl ei arfer yn tacluso'r lle ac yn potsian efo'r peirianna.

"Ie. Beth dych chi isie? O's 'da chi ganiatâd athro i ddod yma?"

"Oes, Mr Edwards. Dw i eisiau gorffen y graff yma i Mr Williams, Maths."

"Dewch imi weld e, te. Mmm. Mr Williams, ife? Mi ga i air 'da fe i weld os ych chi'n gweud y gwir."

"Iawn," atebodd Neil yn eitha hyderus. Celwydd golau ddywedodd o, ac roedd Edwyn IT yn llawer rhy ddiog i fynd i chwilio am Mr Williams, Maths, yn ystod yr awr ginio.

Cyn pen chwinciad, roedd o ar y gadair dro wrth y cyfrifiadur a oedd reit yng nghornel y stafell lle nad oedd modd i neb weld y sgrîn.

Rhif pin. *Password.* Clic *Inbox. Favourites. Messages. Chatroom.* O, gobeithio'i bod Hi yno. Dechreuodd deipio.

'HELO, MERCH Y WE. TI YNA? MEDDWL AMDANAT TI. DDIM YN GALLU GWEITHIO.'

'V VYD. GWRANDO DIM YN Y GWERSI. ARHOLIADAU!!! MEWN CARIAD XXXX.'

'DWI SIO DY WELD DI DYDD SADWRN. LLE???'

'CAFFI GORNEL STRYD. COFFI R US.'

'PRYD?'

'2 O'R GLOCH. XXXXX.'

'XXXXX I T FYD.'

Nos Wener, roedd Neil Llgada Sgwâr yn methu'n lân â chysgu. Roedd o'n troi a throsi â'i feddwl o'n rasio fel car Ferrari. Roedd y Ferch ar y We wedi ei ddal yn ei gwe ac yn mynd rownd a rownd yn ei ben o. Roedd o wedi cynhyrfu'n ofnadwy – yn union fel tasa hi'n ddiwrnod Dolig y diwrnod wedyn, ac ynta fel plentyn bach yn disgwyl cael beic newydd sbon gan Santa drannoeth. Doedd o ddim wedi bod mor gynhyrfus ers y diwrnod y cyrhaeddodd y bocsys a oedd yn dal ei gyfrifiadur newydd. Hwnnw oedd ei gariad cynta ers dwy flynedd bellach. Hwnnw oedd ei gwmni bob bore, bob nos a phob penwythnos ers hynny. Ond, rŵan, roedd o wedi aeddfedu ac ar fin cyfarfod â'i gariad go-iawn cynta. Rhyfedd, meddyliodd, sut roedd ei hen gariad wedi ei gynorthwyo i gael gafael ar gariad newydd.

Chwiliodd am ei drowsus bagi gwyrdd yn y

cwpwrdd dillad glân. Roedd o wedi ei roi i'w fam i'w olchi ers diwrnod neu ddau ond doedd dim golwg ohono. Doedd wahaniaeth – roedd crys melyn Brasil yn lân neis, a gwisgodd hwnnw a'i hen jîns glas. Camodd i'w sgidia dal adar gwyn â thair streipan las a ddangosai eu bod nhw'n rhai da. Roedd o'n teimlo'n rêl boi rŵan a chribodd ei wallt yn y drych uwch ben y lle tân yn y stafell ffrynt. Damia! Ploryn newydd ar ymyl ei ên. Y pump Mars bach 'na a fwytaodd y noson o'r blaen oedd ar fai, mae'n siŵr. Byddai'n rhaid iddo roi'r gorau i sglaffio sothach fel yna o hyn ymlaen.

Roedd y bys i'r dre yn llawn dop, a phawb a oedd yn sefyll yn edrych yn flin ac yn cael eu hysgwyd o gwmpas wrth hongian oddi ar y reilan wrth y to. Roedd o'n rhy gynnar. Edrychodd ar ei oriawr. Roedd o'n llawer rhy gynnar. Ugain munud tan y câi ei chyfarfod Hi – cyfarfod yr un a fu'n mynd rownd a rownd yn ei ben ers wythnosau. Ugain munud arall, a châi weld yr un y rhoddodd gymaint o swsus iddi dros sgrîn ei gyfrifiadur. Swsus electronig yn llithro'n wlyb i lawr y llinellau ffôn ati hi. Ati Hi. Roedd o'n dechrau chwysu, ac aeth i HMV i drio rhoi ei feddwl ar rywbeth arall. Aflwyddiannus. Edrychodd ar ei oriawr. Allai o ddal ei wynt am funud? Munud cyfan? Trïodd. Methodd. Cymerodd fwy o wynt cyn dechrau yr eildro. Llwyddo. Dim ond jyst.

Pum munud i fynd. Cerddodd i mewn dan yr

arwydd Coffee R Us a daeth dynes i ofyn lle i faint oedd arno'i angen.

"I ddau, plîs."

"Iawn. Wrth ymyl y ffenast ta yn y lle smocio yn y cefn?"

"Wrth ymyl y ffenast, plîs."

"Dyna ti. Beth hoffet ti, ta?"

"Un Sprite mawr, plîs."

"Rwbath arall?"

"Dim diolch."

Ddylai o fod wedi aros amdani cyn archebu? Doedd o ddim wedi cyfarfod merch fel hyn o'r blaen. Roedd yn rhaid iddo fo gael rhywbeth ac yntau'n eistedd yn y caffi posh ma. Canodd cloch y drws y tu ôl iddo. Trodd rownd â'i galon yn ei wddf. Cwpl mewn oed. Agorodd y drws eto. Merch? Na. Ifan B! Beth gythral roedd y twmffat hwnnw yn ei wneud yn yr un lle â fo? Doedd o ddim wedi dweud gair wrth neb am hyn. Sbïodd Ifan B yr un mor syn arno fo.

"Be ddiawl… ?"

"Be uffar… ?"

Ifan B ddechreuodd ar ei esboniad. "Dw i'n cyfarfod ffrind yma."

"O. Pwy felly? Sgin ti'm llawer ohonyn nhw… !"

"Rhywun dw i ddim wedi'i gweld o'r blaen."

"Merch felly? A finna… "

Aeth y ddau'n welw. Y we. Roedd y ddau wedi

cyfarfod cariad ar y we! Roeddan nhw wedi trefnu cyfarfod yn yr un caffi ar yr un dydd Sadwrn ar yr un awr o'r dydd. Roedd y peth yn ormod o gyd-ddigwyddiad. Roedd y ddau hefyd wedi bod yn ymddwyn yn rhyfedd am dros ddeufis, a dyna pam – y Ferch ar y We! Pwy oedd hi?

Gwibiodd rhywbeth mawr pinc fel candifflos heibio ffenast Coffee R Us. Nina, yn ei thracsiwt newydd ac ar y *roller-blades* a gafodd hi y Dolig diwethaf.

"Be ti'n da ma? Lle ma Mam a Dad? Efo pwy wyt ti?"

"Maen nhw ar eu ffordd. Dim ond galw heibio nes i i ddweud, 'lot o swsus gen i a Merch y We!'"

Sbïodd Neil ac Ifan B yn syn ar ei gilydd. Allai hyn ddim bod yn wir… Nina oedd Merch y We! Cododd y ddau. Roedd Nina'n bomio mynd i lawr y stryd cyn iddyn nhw ddod dros y sioc. Sgrialodd y ddau ar ei hôl. Yn ei frys, anghofiodd Neil dalu am ei Sprite.

Tu allan i'r cylch
gan Gwion Hallam

Maen nhw'n dweud bod na drysor ym mhen draw'r enfys. Cyfle i ennill y loteri heb wario'r un bunt. Jacpot o aur i bwy bynnag sydd â digon o amser i chwilio amdano.

Roedd digonedd o amser gan Delyth ond nid oedd hi'n chwilio am ddim byd. Roedd hi'n crwydro trwy'r parc ar y ffordd adre o'r ysgol, yn dilyn ei thrwyn heb frys i gyrraedd nôl i dŷ gwag, a sylwodd hi ddim ar yr enfys yn hanner cylch perffaith o liwiau. Cyd-ddigwyddiad, o bosib, ond dyna pryd y daeth hi o hyd i'r trysor wedi ei lapio a'i guddio mewn parsel bach twt. Trysor arswydus o drist.

Mae bron pawb wedi clywed am Noa. Mae gan ambell un gof Ysgol Sul am yr enfys ar ddiwedd y stori. Enfys yn arwydd bod y glaw wedi cilio. Dim felly'r pnawn hwnnw. Wrth i Delyth gerdded trwy'r parc, roedd y glaw'n parhau i ddisgyn a gwlychu ei gwallt a chasglu yn yr hwd ar ei chefn. Pam mynd i drafferth i'w wisgo fe nawr? Roedd ei gwallt yn wlyb domen wedi iddi dreulio'r awr ginio yn cerdded o gwmpas yr iard. Dim ond ei gwlychu a wnâi'r glaw, ac roedd hynny'n well na bod i mewn gyda'r plant eraill.

'Del' fyddai ei mam yn ei galw. 'Del' fyddai pawb yn ei galw ddwy flynedd yn ôl yn Ysgol Gynradd Bryn Pwll. 'Del' yn lle 'Delyth'. Byddai hyd yn oed Mr Maloney, prifathro'r ysgol, yn ei galw hi'n 'Del' ar adegau. Byddai hynny'n gwneud iddi chwerthin bob amser. Prifathro'r ysgol yn ei galw hi'n 'Del', fel tase fe'n ddim mwy na ffrind! Byddai ei ffrindiau hi i gyd yn ei galw hi'n 'Del' ddwy flynedd yn ôl – cyn i Karen benderfynu nad oedd hi yn ddel. 'Del Not' oedd hi nawr. 'Del Not' fyddai'r plant yn yr ysgol i gyd yn ei galw.

Beth dynnodd ei sylw yn y parc y diwrnod hwnnw? Daeth rhywbeth fel cysgod i dorri ar draws llif ei meddyliau. Efallai iddi glywed sŵn gwichian o'r coed? Pesychiad bach ofnus? Beth bynnag y rheswm, fe stopiodd hi ar ganol y llwybr ac edrych i'r chwith i ganol y brigau a'r drysni. Wedi meddwl am eiliad, fe gamodd i gyfeiriad y coed. Dylai fod wedi mynd â ffrind gyda hi. Fyddai hi ddim mor ofnus â chwmni ganddi.

Roedd ganddi hi ffrindiau, wrth gwrs. Plant o'r un ysgol. Plant o'r un dosbarth. Plant oedd, o wythnos i wythnos, yn mynd i'r un gwersi â hi – fel Mair Owen Pritchard, a fu'n eistedd wrth ei hymyl hi am awr y pnawn hwnnw. Wrth ochr Mair Owen Pritchard y byddai hi'n eistedd yn y gwersi Mathemateg bob tro. Dyna oedd trefn Mr Jones, Maths. Fe oedd yr unig athro yr oedd pawb yn ei ofni. Yr unig athro oedd yn mynnu bod pawb yn eistedd wrth yr un desgiau bob tro. Roedd hi'n ddiolchgar am hynny am ei bod hi'n cael eistedd wrth ochr Mair. Roedd hi'n hoff iawn o Mair ac roedd Mair Owen Pritchard yn siarad â hi weithiau. "Rwber neis. Ga i ei fenthyg e?" gofynnodd Mair iddi y pnawn hwnnw ac, ar ddiwedd y wers, fe gadwodd hi'r rwber gan ddweud bod arni eisiau ei fenthyg e eto, tan y diwrnod wedyn. "Wrth gwrs," meddai Delyth. Roedd hi'n hapus bod Mair yn ffrind iddi o gwbwl. Roedd hi'n credu bod Mair Owen Pritchard yn ferch hynod o glyfar – yn wahanol iddi hi ei hun.

Nid ei bod hi'n ferch dwp, nac araf. A dweud y gwir, roedd hi'n well am wneud syms na sawl un yn y dosbarth. Roedd hi'n well efo rhifau nag efo geiriau, ac efallai bod hynny'n esbonio pam na chafodd hi flas ar y wers y pnawn hwnnw. Gwers Mathemateg heb rifau! Y cwbwl wnaeth Mr Jones ar ddechrau'r wers oedd tynnu llun cylchoedd ar y bwrdd gwyn. Tri chylch mawr yr un maint a oedd yn cyffwrdd â'i gilydd – yn croesi'i gilydd – ar ganol y bwrdd. Dywedodd mai rhyw fath o ddeiagramau oedden nhw. Doedd hi ddim yn cofio'n iawn, ond roedd hi'n cofio ond yn rhy dda bod enwau ym mhob cylch. Enwau plant y dosbarth i gyd fel mewn rhestr, ond eu bod wedi eu rhoi yn y cylchoedd priodol bob tro – pob enw yn perthyn i rywbeth. Achos roedd pob un o'r cylchoedd yn cynrychioli gweithgaredd, neu ryw fath o grŵp. Cylch rygbi a phêl-rwyd oedd y cylch cynta. Cylch y côr oedd yr ail, a chylch yr ysgol i gyd oedd y trydydd. Roedd pawb yn perthyn i'r cylch hwnnw.

A dyna'r darn cymhleth – wel, i'r rhan fwya yn y dosbarth. Gan fod y cylchoedd yn croesi'i gilydd – yn gorgyffwrdd â'i gilydd – roedd rhai disgyblion yn gallu perthyn i ddau gylch, neu hyd yn oed i'r tri. Disgyblion fel Mair Owen Pritchard. Roedd hi'n chwarae pêl-rwyd ac yn canu yn y côr ac, fel pawb arall, roedd hi'n perthyn i gylch yr ysgol hefyd. Roedd enw Mair reit ynghanol y bwrdd efo pedwar enw arall tra oedd y lleill yn perthyn i ddau gylch o leia. Roedd rhai o'r bechgyn yn chwarae rygbi ac yn perthyn i gylch yr ysgol, neu'n canu'n y côr ac yn ddisgyblion yn yr ysgol. A rhai o'r merched yn chwarae pêl-rwyd ac yn ddisgyblion yn yr ysgol. Roedd pawb – fel hi, Delyth – yn perthyn i gylch ysgol, wrth gwrs. Pawb yn saff o gael eu henwi ar y siart. Dyna pam roedd Mr Jones wedi rhoi 'yr ysgol' yn thema i'r trydydd cylch, er mwyn gwneud yn siŵr bod enw pob plentyn yn cael ei gynnwys. Nid oedd Delyth yn canu yn y côr nac yn chwarae pêl-rwyd, ond roedd hi'n perthyn i gylch yr ysgol. Roedd hi'n hapus ei bod hi'n perthyn yn rhywle.

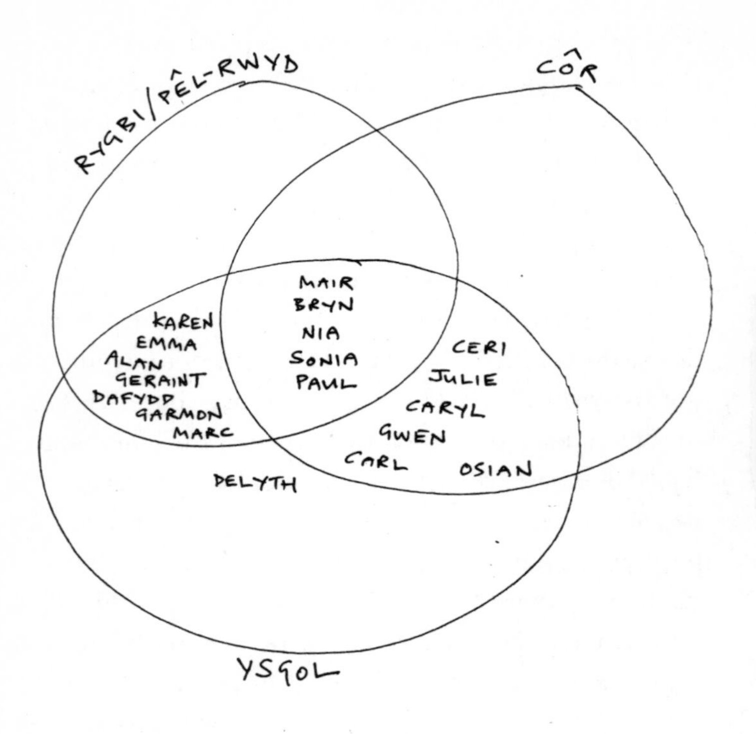

Beth oedd diben y peth? Dywedodd Mr Jones y byddai rhifau yn y cylchoedd y tro nesa. Efallai y gwnâi hynny fwy o synnwyr i Delyth. Efallai mai rhif un fyddai hi. Wedi'r cwbwl, dim ond hi oedd yno ar ei phen ei hun mewn un cylch.

Felly yr oedd hi yn y parc hefyd. Ynghanol cylch bach o goed. Ond doedd hi ddim ar ei phen ei hun erbyn hyn. Roedd hi'n sefyll uwch ben parsel – yn rhyfeddu, yn synnu at y bocs wrth ei thraed. Plygodd i lawr i gael gweld beth oedd yno cyn codi eto er mwyn cael golwg iawn ar wyneb y babi. Babi mewn bocs â chot law wedi ei gosod yn sydyn ofalus ar y brigau uwch ei ben. Babi wedi ei lapio a'i adael gan fam a oedd yn sâl – yn gofidio, falle? Yn methu dygymod? Newydd ei adael funudau'n ôl. Dim mwy na rhyw awr. Roedd yn cysgu o hyd, heb wybod am y byd a'i broblemau.

"Paid â deffro, paid â deffro. Dere gartre da fi," meddai Del wrth ei godi'n ofalus o'r bocs a'i osod e'n saff ym mhlygiadau ei chot. Ei guddio'n ofalus o'r golwg. Wrth gerdded yn gyflym o gysgod y coed, wnaeth hi ddim sylwi ar yr enfys yn wên ben i waered ar fyd a oedd wedi'i droi â'i ben i lawr.

Petaen nhw ond yn cyrraedd y tŷ, byddai popeth yn iawn. Neb yno i'w croesawu nhw nôl. Neb i fusnesu, gan fod babi arall yn fwy pwysig i'w mam. Babi Linda, chwaer Delyth. Roedd ei mam mwy neu lai wedi symud i fyw i dŷ Linda. Roedd hi'n gwarchod o hyd gan fod honno wedi mynd nôl i'w gwaith. Roedd Delyth yn gorfod edrych ar ei hôl ei hun. Ac roedd hi'n gwneud hynny'n iawn. Gallai hi ofalu am y babi a oedd wedi ei guddio yn ei chot. Pum munud bach eto ac fe fydden nhw gartre. Yn saff lle na allai pobol eu gweld.

"Paid â deffro, mach i. Cei di ddeffro pan fyddwn ni gartre."

"Del Not! Be ti'n neud?" Daeth y llais o'r tu ôl iddi. "Gyda pwy wyt ti'n siarad? Ti dy hunan?!"

Mae'n rhyfedd sut y bydd pobol yn dewis eich nabod chi weithiau. Karen Jenkins oedd yno – un na fyddai'n trafferthu siarad â Delyth o gwbwl fel arfer.

"Pobol dost sy'n gneud ny. A be sy da ti fan na?" holodd wrth iddi sylwi ar fol Delyth.

"Dim byd," atebodd Del.

"Ond ti'n edrych fel se ti'n disgwyl!" meddai Karen yn goeglyd, heb feddwl am funud ei bod hi mor agos at y gwir.

"Cario dillad, na'i gyd."

"Cario dillad o le?! Wedi eu dwgyd nhw wyt ti?"

"Cario dillad i ffrind!" meddai Delyth, gan wybod na fyddai'n credu'r fath beth.

"Pa ffrind?! Be sy da ti i gwato, Del Not? Gad fi i weld be sy da ti yn dy got," mynnodd Karen. Ac, ar hynny, pwniodd fol Delyth. Gollyngodd y babi floedd uchel a dechrau crio. Dechreuodd Del gerdded i ffwrdd yn gyflym.

"Ma da ti fabi dan dy got!" ebychodd Karen pan fedrodd hi siarad o'r diwedd. "Ma da ti fabi, Del Not!"

"Ac mae e'n bert fel ei fam!" galwodd Delyth yn ôl wrth groesi'r ffordd i gyfeiriad ei thŷ.

"Ond babi pwy yw e, Delyth? Babi pwy sy da ti fan na? Pam ti'n ei guddio fe?"

Rhuthrodd Del i ffwrdd rywsut rhwng cerdded a rhedeg. Sgipiodd fel plentyn heb edrych yn ôl a welodd hi mo Karen yn anelu at y ciosg gerllaw.

Ond doedd Delyth ddim yn dwp. Wnaeth hi ddim dilyn ei llwybr arferol i'r tŷ rhag ofn y byddai Karen wedi ei dilyn hi yno neu wedi ffonio ei mam yn nhŷ Linda. Aeth hi ddim adre o gwbwl. Trodd yn ôl am y dre heb wybod yn iawn lle i fynd. Aeth heibio'r siopau a'r tafarndai, a drws ochr y Bull – tafarn dawela'r dre, lle y gweithiai ei thad cyn y ddamwain. Llonyddodd y babi eto yng nghynhesrwydd ei chot. Erbyn hynny, roedd hi nôl wrth yr ysgol. A dyna lle y safodd am sbel wrth y gatiau agored, heb unman i fynd. Safodd yn stond cyn pwyso ar y wal a sylwi bod y glaw wedi peidio. Roedd hi wedi ymlâdd. Gwyliodd gar heddlu'n mynd heibio am ganol y dre.

Daeth hi'n amlwg i Delyth nad oedd unman y gallai fynd ond am yr ysgol. Roedd y gatiau ar agor fel petaen nhw'n ei gwahodd hi, a sylwodd fod golau yn y neuadd. Cododd ei llygaid at ffenestri'r ystafelloedd dosbarth uwchben. I gyfeiriad yr ystafell lle y bu hi ychydig oriau cynt yn y wers Fathemateg. Ai honna oedd y ffenest? Roedd hi'n anodd dyfalu'n iawn o'r tu allan. Byddai'n rhaid mynd i mewn i gael gweld.

Hanner awr wedyn, daeth yr heddlu'n ôl at yr ysgol. I mewn i'r maes parcio ac i'r neuadd a oedd yn olau o hyd. Nid oedd Bobi'r gofalwr wedi gweld na chlywed unrhyw un o gwbwl, a fyddai neb wedi medru ei basio chwaith. Pwysleisiodd fod yr ysgol yn wag. Ond aeth yr heddlu i chwilio ac i agor pob drws beth bynnag; i daflu golwg ym mhob ystafell ddosbarth. Nes cyrraedd y bloc Mathemateg.

Nid oedd golwg o Delyth, ond roedd y babi'n ddiogel. Wedi ei lapio a'i adael yn saff o dan ddesg Mr Jones. Diolch byth iddo grio pan agorodd y plismon y drws. Fe'i clywodd a galw ar ei bartner.

Dau funud o chwilio. Gwneud yn siŵr nad oedd Delyth yn y dosbarth o hyd. A gadawodd y plismyn heb sylwi ar y bwrdd gwyn ar y wal. Y bwrdd gwyn lle roedd cylchoedd. Tri chylch yr un maint. Ac enw wedi ei ychwanegu at y trydydd cylch. 'BABI DEL'.

Cylch tân
gan Meinir Eluned Jones

Eisteddai Myrddin yn yr ystafell aros. Roedd cymysgedd rhyfedd o nerfusrwydd a chynnwrf yn llifo trwy'i wythiennau. Edrychodd ar y cloc: deg munud i bedwar. Doedd y cyfarfod gyda'r uwch-arolygydd ddim i gychwyn tan bedwar, ond roedd wedi cyrraedd bum munud ar hugain yn gynnar am nad oedd am wneud argraff wael a hefyd am na allai ddioddef disgwyl yn hwy.

Bu'n gweithio fel diffoddwr tân yn yr un orsaf ers ugain mlynedd. Roedd wedi achub cannoedd o fywydau. Ymsythodd wrth gofio'r eitem ar y newyddion a'r lluniau yn y papurau newydd. Roedd y ffaith iddo achub bywyd yr Aelod Seneddol pan oedd ei gartref yn wenfflam wedi'i wneud yn arwr cenedlaethol. Cafodd wobr am ei ddewrder, ond nid dyrchafiad – am ei fod yn rhy ifanc ar y pryd, mae'n debyg. Nawr, ac yntau'n ddwy a deugain, roedd ar yr uwch-arolygydd eisiau ei weld!

Pan gafodd wybod am y cyfarfod y dydd Llun cynt, roedd braidd yn ofnus. Mae'n rhyfedd sut mae rhywun wastad yn fwy parod i wynebu ffrae na chanmoliaeth. Ond pan soniodd wrth Nerys, ei wraig, nos Lun, disgynnodd y darnau i'w lle. Roedd ar fin cael dyrchafiad! Trodd ei olygon oddi wrth y bwrdd bwyd ac at gynnwys y ffrâm ar wal y gegin: *'Daily Mirror, April 11, 1992 : Welsh Merlin Saves MP.'*

Pa ddiwrnod roedd o i ymweld â'r uwch-arolygydd? Ebrill yr unfed ar ddeg! Trodd at Gwawr a Rhys.

"Sut hoffach chi fynd ar wylia go-iawn yr ha yma? Ddim i Ben Llŷn at Taid a Nain, ond i Disney World!" Edrychodd y ddau ar eu tad yn llawn edmygedd, cyn dechrau bloeddio a chanu. "A be am dŷ newydd crand yn rhywle fel Coedlan yr Helyg, efo gardd fawr yn y cefn, a wardrob fawr y galli di gerdded i mewn iddi?" Taflodd winc ar Nerys.

Roedd pob sgwrs yn y tŷ am weddill yr wythnos yn troi o gwmpas cynlluniau'r teulu wedi i Myrddin gael dyrchafiad.

Doedd ar Myrddin ddim eisiau sôn am y peth gyda'i gydweithwyr hyd nes byddai popeth wedi'i gadarnhau'n swyddogol. Ond, roedd yn rhaid iddo ddweud wrth Gareth. Roedd y ddau wedi bod yn ffrindiau pennaf ers dyddiau ysgol gynradd ac wedi dechrau gweithio yn yr un orsaf dân ar yr un pryd. Byddai'r ddau deulu'n mynd draw i dai ei gilydd am brydau bwyd yn wythnosol, a'r plant yn ffrindiau hefyd. Yn ôl Rhys a Tomos, y ddau frawd bach busneslyd, roedd lle i gredu bod Gwawr ac Ifan, mab Gareth, yn gariadon. Roedd Gareth yn falch iawn o glywed bod ei ffrind gorau ar fin cael dyrchafiad, a bu ef a'i wraig, Rhiannon – a Nerys, wrth gwrs – wrthi'n trefnu parti sypreis i Myrddin. A Myrddin yn chwarae'r gêm gan gogio nad oedd wedi deall dim.

"Mae Mr Jones yn barod i'ch gweld chi rŵan," meddai'r ysgrifenyddes. Safodd Myrddin a sythu ei dei. Cnociodd ar y drws yn gadarn a chymryd anadl ddofn cyn cerdded i mewn i'r ystafell. Bu yma unwaith o'r blaen, ddeng mlynedd yn ôl, pan gafodd ei longyfarch am achub bywyd yr Aelod Seneddol, ond roedd yr ystafell mor wahanol erbyn hyn, gyda'r dodrefn newydd a'r cyfrifiaduron modern.

"Mr Hughes… Myrddin… rydych chi wedi bod yn gweithio'n yr orsaf ma ers tro… "

"Ugain mlynedd mis nesa, Syr. Nid mod i'n sgota am barti!"

"Ia." Anesmwythodd yr uwch-arolygydd yn ei gadair. "Mi ydach chi'n gwybod bod y llywodraeth wedi bod yn recriwtio mwy o fechgyn ifanc i ddod i mewn i'r gwaith ma'n ddiweddar… "

"Dwi di gweld yr hysbysebion ar y bocs. Yr hogyn cw – Rhys, te – yn brolio wrth pawb yn rysgol mai'i dad o ydi'r dyn mawr efo'r mysyls sy'n achub y flondan na o'r fflama. Plant, te? Wela i o'r llun bod gynnoch chitha blant. 'Wrach y medrwn ni neud rwbath fel dau deulu rwbryd? Pryd o fwyd yn 'yn lle ni? Ma'r misus yn giamstar ar neud sdêc. Dw inna'n reit dda ar y barbeciw hefyd. Nid mod i'n brolio, te!"

"Hm. Fy wyrion i ydi'r rhain," atebodd yr uwch-arolygydd, â'i dôn mor wahanol i barablu Myrddin. "Yr hyn dwi'n drio'i ddweud ydi bod y rhaglen recriwtio wedi bod yn llwyddiant mawr, a bod 'na gynnydd o wyth deg y cant yn y rhai sydd wedi cwblhau'r cwrs hyfforddi leni o'i gymharu â ffigyrau'r pum mlynedd diwethaf... "

"Iesgob! Da, ynte? Dwi wastad wedi deud y bysa hi'n rheitiach i hogia ifanc ddŵad i weithio i le fel hyn, a gwneud job go iawn, yn hytrach na chladdu'u trwyna mewn rhyw hen lyfra yn y colega ma. Dydi o'm yn iach, nac ydi, yr holl ddarllen ma?"

"MR HUGHES!" Cododd yr uwch-arolygydd ei lais, "Wnewch chi, plîs, adael i mi orffen yr hyn sy gen i'w ddweud? Mae hi'n ddigon anodd fel mae hi! Rydan ni wedi derbyn saith gweithiwr newydd i'r orsaf yma. Criw da a dderbyniodd raddau uchel iawn yn y cwrs hyfforddi. Ond gan bod angen lle iddyn nhw – a'r gwaith yn debygol o gynnwys agweddau a fyddai'n eich diflasu chi, fel *financial balance* â ballu – mae'n rhaid i ni golli dau weithiwr presennol. Doedd hi ddim yn hawdd penderfynu pwy fyddai'n gadael, ond, yn seiliedig ar ganlyniadau'r profion ffitrwydd, mae arna i ofn y bydd yn rhaid i ni'ch colli chi. Mae'n ddrwg calon gen i. Mi fedrwn ni gynnig pensiwn da i chi, ac, os gwnewch chi adael cyn diwedd wythnos nesaf, mi rown ni chwe mis o gyflog i chi."

Roedd Myrddin wedi'i syfrdanu. Roedd cymaint o gwestiynau yn llenwi ei feddwl. Cymaint o bethau nad oedd yn gwneud synnwyr. Roedd o'n ddyn tân da. Y gorau. Roedd y tapiau newyddion ganddo i brofi hynny. Roedd ei ben yn llawn marciau cwestiwn mawr duon ar gefndir gwag. Wyddai o ddim am ddim ond am ddiffodd tân. Ers pan oedd o'n hogyn bach, roedd wedi bod yn breuddwydio am ddringo ysgolion uchel a diffodd fflamau gwyllt gyda phibell ddŵr.

O blith yr holl gwestiynau dyrys a oedd ar ei feddwl, mynnodd ofyn pwy oedd y gweithiwr arall a fyddai'n gorfod gadael.

"Cyril Parry. Mi oedd o'n ymddeol Dolig beth bynnag. Mae'n ddrwg calon gen i, Myrddin."

Aeth o ddim adre ar ei union gan nad oedd yn barod i wynebu ei deulu a thorri'r newydd annisgwyl iddynt. Aeth am dro ar hyd y traeth gan gicio tywod o'i flaen a sathru cregyn a gwylio'r gwylanod yn plymio i'r môr i hel pysgod. Edrychodd ar ei oriawr: hanner awr wedi chwech. Roedd hi wedi dechrau tywyllu hefyd. Gwell iddo fynd adref. Sut yn y byd y gallai dorri'r newydd i'r teulu a datgan mai Pen Llŷn fyddai hi eleni eto, a hwythau wedi edrych ymlaen gymaint at fynd i Disney World?

Gyrrodd ar hyd y stryd at y tŷ. Roedd pobman yn dywyll. Roedd yn falch nad oedd neb adref er mwyn iddo gael amser i feddwl.

Agorodd y drws a cherdded i mewn i'r ystafell fyw. Estynnodd am y swits golau, a... 'BANG! BANG! BANG!'

"Sypreis!"

Drwy fwg y *party poppers* a'r holl falŵns, gallai weld saith person yn sefyll o'i flaen wedi gwisgo'n barod am barti. Ei deulu ef a theulu Gareth.

"Llongyfarchiadau, Dad!" Rhedodd y plant ato a'i gofleidio. Daeth Nerys ato gyda gwydryn o siampén yn ei llaw a phlannu clamp o gusan ar ei foch.

Wyddai Myrddin ddim beth i'w ddweud. Roedd yr ystafell fyw yn llawn cerddoriaeth a chynnwrf, balŵns a bwydydd o bob math. Pawb yn lliwgar ac yn llawen. Pawb wedi mynd i drafferth. Allai o ddim dweud y gwir. Dim rŵan, a diflasu pawb.

"Diolch," meddai gan ddrachtio'r siampén a gwenu'n glên ar bawb.

Roedd hi'n anodd iddo, yn enwedig pan ofynnodd Gareth beth yn union oedd gan yr uwch-arolygydd i'w ddweud.

"O, ti'n gwybod, jest dweud mod i wedi cael dyrchafiad. Fawr o'm byd, a deud y gwir."

Sut fath o ateb oedd peth felly? Wrth gwrs, pe byddai Myrddin yn dweud y gwir, byddai'n ailadrodd pob gair ac yn dramateiddio popeth hefyd. Ond, yn ffodus, cyn i Gareth sylwi, bloeddiodd y ddau frawd bach eu bod wedi gweld Gwawr ac Ifan yn cusanu ar y patio. Carwriaeth y ddau, ac nid 'dyrchafiad' Myrddin, oedd canolbwynt y parti wedi hynny. Eisteddodd yntau ar y soffa'n dawel.

Y noson honno, methai Myrddin â chysgu. Teimlai'n flin ei fod yn cael ei orfodi i adael swydd yr oedd yn ei charu, a theimlai'n euog am dwyllo'i deulu a'i ffrind pennaf.

Bu'n gorwedd yn llonydd yn syllu ar y nenfwd am hydoedd, yn ceisio meddwl sut i esbonio i bawb beth oedd wedi digwydd go-iawn. Yna, cafodd syniad. Nid oedd dim amdani ond torri'r cylch a phrofi ei ddewrder a'i ymroddiad unwaith eto.

Sleifiodd o'r gwely, gan ofalu peidio â deffro Nerys. Cipiodd ei ddillad a cherdded i lawr y grisiau yn ddistaw bach. Yno, yn yr ystafell fyw dywyll, ynghanol olion y parti, gwisgodd amdano a cherdded i'r sied yn yr ardd gefn. Estynnodd am y fflachlamp, y can petrol a'r ffon fesur olew. Aeth yn ôl i'r gegin ac estyn blwch matsys a oedd yn cael ei gadw wrth ymyl y popty. A gadawodd y tŷ.

Am y tro cynta y diwrnod hwnnw, roedd popeth yn glir yn ei feddwl. Cerddodd drwy'r dref yn llechwraidd rhag ofn i rywun ei adnabod, ond doedd neb o gwmpas beth bynnag.

Cyrhaeddodd y tai crand, daith pum munud o'i gartref ei hun, ond eto mor wahanol. Rhif 15. Cofiai'r tŷ'n iawn. Tŷ'r Aelod Seneddol. Roedd y gwaith atgyweirio costus wedi cuddio unrhyw ôl o ddinistr y tân a fu yno ddeng mlynedd ynghynt.

Roedd Myrddin yn adnabod yr adeilad yn dda. Aeth i mewn yr un ffordd ag o'r blaen, pan ddringodd drwy ffenestr y gegin i achub yr Aelod Seneddol o'r tân. Doedd dim angen torri'r un cwarel; gallai ddadfachu'r ffenestr gyda'r ffon fesur olew.

Eiliadau yn ddiweddarach, safai yn sinc yr Aelod Seneddol. Pe na byddai mor nerfus ac mor benderfynol o achub ei swydd, byddai wedi gweld y sefyllfa'n ddoniol – fo, Myrddin Hughes, yn sefyll yn sinc cegin rhyw wleidydd pwysig! Ond, roedd amser yn brin, ac roedd yn rhaid iddo frysio. Camodd ar flaenau ei draed i'r ystafell fyw anferth. Estynnodd am yr hen gadair eisteddfodol. Roedd arogl polish drud ar y pren derw. Doedd gan Myrddin fawr i'w ddweud wrth feirdd na'u cadeiriau, felly safodd ar y gadair yn ei esgidiau budr. Uwchben y gadair roedd y larwm tân; agorodd ef a thynnu'r batri ohono.

Agorodd y can petrol a thywallt yr hylif dros y carped, y dodrefn a'r cyrtans, gan ofalu peidio â cholli defnyn arno'i hun. Aeth nôl at y drws a gysylltai'r ystafell fyw â'r gegin. Taniodd fatsen a'i thaflu ar lawr. Cydiodd y fflam yn syth. Arhosodd o ddim i weld y fflamau.

Rhedodd yr holl ffordd adref. Roedd amser yn brin iawn. Cyrhaeddodd y tŷ. Rhoddodd y blwch matsys yn ôl wrth y popty a'r ffon fesur olew a'r can petrol gwag yn ôl yn y sied.

Canodd y ffôn gan ddeffro pawb. Atebodd Myrddin ef, gan ofalu ei fod yn swnio'n gysglyd. Yr orsaf oedd yno, yn gofyn am gefnogaeth ychwanegol i ddiffodd tân mawr yn 15 Coedlan yr Helyg. Roedd ei gynllun yn llwyddo.

Carlamodd i lawr y grisiau, a chan ei fod yn ei ddillad o hyd, roedd allan o'r tŷ ac yn ei gar mewn amrantiad.

Roedd mwg trwchus a fflamau gwyllt yn amgylchynu'r tŷ. Aeth Myrddin at un o'r injans, casglu dillad gwrth-dân a phibell ddŵr, cyn mentro at ffenestr y gegin. Roedd dau ddiffoddwr tân yn ymladd y fflamau yn yr ystafell fyw. Amneidiodd Myrddin i ddangos ei fod am fynd i fyny'r grisiau, a daeth un ohonyn nhw gydag o.

Roedd yr Aelod Seneddol a'i wraig yn sefyll wrth ffenestr eu hystafell wely yn galw'n wyllt am help, a phlancedi dros eu cegau a'u trwynau rhag anadlu mwg, ond roedd y ffenestr yn rhy boeth i'w hagor. Gyda'i fenyg arbennig, gallai Myrddin wneud hyn yn rhwydd.

Mewn dim o dro, roedd ysgol wrth y ffenestr a dringodd yr Aelod Seneddol allan i ddiogelwch yr ambiwlans. Roedd ei wraig yn rhy ofnus i fynd ei hun, felly cariodd Myrddin hi, gan wybod gystal llun a wnâi hwnnw i'r papurau newydd. Ac yntau newydd gyrraedd y ddaear, gwelodd y diffoddwr tân a oedd yn yr ystafell fyw yn rhedeg allan o'r tŷ. "Pawb o'r ffordd!" gwaeddodd. Ffrwydrodd yr adeilad. Tasgodd darnau miniog o wydr chwilboeth y ffenestri a'r llechi oddi ar y to i bobman, gan anafu llawer.

Yn ddiweddarach, yn yr ysbyty, daeth yr Uwch-Arolygydd Morgan Jones at wely Myrddin.

"Gobeithio na chawsoch chi ormod o anaf."

"Na – dwi'n rêl boi, diolch. Chydig o friwiau, dyna i gyd. Dywedwch wrtha i – sut mae o?"

"Mae Geraint Powell – a Mrs Powell – yn holliach, Myrddin. Diolch i chi, wrth gwrs; mi wnaethoch chi weithredu'n arwrol iawn heno. Mae dynion y papurau newydd yn galw am eich gweld chi'n barod."

Roedd y cynllwyn wedi gweithio, a Myrddin yn arwr cenedlaethol unwaith eto! Llanwodd ei galon â balchder.

"Ond, mae gen i newyddion drwg, mae arna i ofn. Nid chi oedd yr unig ddiffoddwr tân fentrodd i fyny'r grisiau heno… " Wrth gwrs! Roedd Myrddin wedi anghofio popeth am y dyn arall. "Mi fu Gareth Francis farw yn y ffrwydriad."

Gareth! Trodd stumog Myrddin. Roedd o wedi lladd ei ffrind pennaf! Roedd o wedi lladd Gareth er mwyn cadw ei waith.

Roedd y cylch wedi cau amdano, ond wedi chwyddo tu hwnt i bob rheolaeth hefyd. Roedd yn ddu un funud, yn wyn y munud wedyn, yna'n goch tanllyd. Dychmygodd glywed sgrechiadau Gareth yn atseinio'n ei ben. Y boen, y dadrith, y ffaith ei fod o, Myrddin, yn llofrudd. Roedd y cylch yn agor a chau mor gyflym, nes codi chwildod a chyfog. Roedd yn rhaid iddo adael yr ysbyty. Roedd yn rhaid iddo ddianc a thorri ffiniau'r cylch.

'Myrddin does a disappearing act after suspicious fire.'

Codai'r erthygl lu o gwestiynau ynglŷn â'r tân a rôl Myrddin yn y digwyddiad, a thalai deyrnged i ddewrder diamheuol y Swyddog Gareth Francis. Gareth Francis, a ddyrchafwyd yn ddiweddar ac a oedd wedi bwriadu prynu tŷ newydd iddo ef, ei wraig, a'u dau o blant y drws nesaf i dŷ'r Aelod Seneddol yng Nghoedlan yr Helyg.

Diflannodd Myrddin oddi ar wyneb y ddaear.

pen dafad

Bach y Nyth
Nia Jones 0 86243 700 8

Cawl Lloerig
Nia Royles (gol.) 0 86243 702 4

Ceri Grafu
Bethan Gwanas 0 86243 692 3

Gwerth y Byd
Mari Rhian Owen 0 86243 703 2

Iawn Boi? ;-)
Caryl Lewis 0 86243 699 0

Jibar
Bedwyr Rees 0 86243 691 5

Mewn Limbo
Gwyneth Glyn 0 86243 693 1

Noson Boring i Mewn
Alun Jones (gol.) 0 86243 701 6

Am wybodaeth am holl gyhoeddiadau'r Lolfa, mynnwch gopi o'n Catalog newydd, neu hwyliwch i mewn i'n gwefan:
www.ylolfa.com

y Lolfa

Talybont, Ceredigion SY24 5AP
e-bost ylolfa@ylolfa.com
gwefan www.ylolfa.com
ffôn +44 (0)1970 832 304
ffacs 832 782
isdn 832 813